BALKRISHNA DOSHI
WRITINGS ON ARCHITECTURE & IDENTITY

BALKRISHNA DOSHI
WRITINGS ON ARCHITECTURE & IDENTITY

EDITED BY VERA SIMONE BADER

TABLE OF CONTENTS

8   The Fabrication of Thoughts and Ideas through Writing
by Vera Simone Bader

16   Interview with Balkrishna Doshi
by Vera Simone Bader, 2019

Writings on Architecture & Identity by Balkrishna Doshi

34   Regionality, 1960

42   Indian Architecture and Its Criticism, 1965

48   Rural Housing, 1970

54   Values and Scales. Musings of an Architect, 1974

66   Limits of City Growth, 1978

74   Architecture and Attitudes, 1979

100   Toward an Appropriate Living Environment, 1980

110   Identity in Architecture, 1981

120   Vohra Houses in Gujarat, 1984

134   Cultural Continuum and Regional Identity in Architecture, 1985

148   Learning from Old Jaipur, 1987

168   Between Notion and Reality, 1989

182   Growth, Change and Development in Urban Centres, 1996

190   Le Corbusier: The Indian Incarnation, 1996

206   Give Time a Break, 1998

THE FABRICATION OF THOUGHTS AND IDEAS THROUGH WRITING

BY VERA SIMONE BADER

Since 1953, Balkrishna Doshi has written up to 12 diaries each year. In his self-designed home in Ahmedabad, the Kamala House, built of concrete, brick and wood, he keeps well over 500 of these handwritten books – full of thoughts on architecture and urban planning, on philosophy and religion, on tradition and modernism. An equal number of sketches of architectural details and cityscapes, as well as animals, people and religious images fill the pages. The diaries alone testify to the tremendous significance of both writing and drawing in his oeuvre, and they vividly demonstrate that, far beyond architecture, Doshi is interested in life and its multifaceted forms. For him, there is a living correlation between writing, drawing and finally, designing. It happens alongside and with each other, and in its very different forms represents the transition from the intuitive to the concrete.

Balkrishna Doshi was born in 1927 in Pune, India. He first began studying architecture in Bombay and in 1951 he started to attending evening courses at the Royal Institute of British Architects (RIBA) in London, where he continued his initiated education. In 1951, he participated in the CIAM congress, 'The Heart of the City', a platform for many of the most famous European architects whom Doshi met for the first time. Among them was Le Corbusier, who was working on the design for the new Indian capital Chandigarh. Doshi was to spend four years in Le Corbusier's Paris office where he learned planning principles before taking over the site management for the three Le Corbusier-designed villas in Ahmedabad. Even today Doshi remembers how greatly he was affected by his experience during this time and later, by his numerous meetings with this renowned theorist and architect of the 20th century. His conversations with Le Corbusier inspired Doshi to reflect on topics such as proportions, movement in space and radicalism in architectural thinking. Years later, he had an equally important exchange with the American architect Louis I. Kahn, whom he convinced in 1962 to design the Indian Institute of Management (IIM) in Ahmedabad. Kahn's play with light and shadow and geometrical forms was to have a profound impact on Doshi's own work.[1]

---

1 B. Doshi, *Paths Uncharted,* Ahmedabad, Vastushilpa Foundation for Studies and Research in Environmental Design, 2011, p. 26ff.

In 1956, Doshi also opened his own architectural office in Ahmedabad. He quickly realised that although he was influenced by the works of Western architects, he had to find his own architectural language that reflected his very personal experiences. His childhood memories of his own family house still serve him as motivation in dealing with Indian architectural culture in lively and innovative ways. He experienced the feeling of a house growing organically, changing and renewing together with the needs of its inhabitants for generations.[2] Doshi increasingly dealt with the vernacular, 'virgin' buildings of the country, untouched by political influences, in order to be able to counteract the globalised architecture which arose in those years.[3] Doshi was not alone in the related search for local identity. After India achieved independence in 1947 this search became even more relevant. There was an entire generation of architects, including Charles Correa, Raj Rewal and Achyut Kanvinde, who had to face the question of how to continue after the British colonialisation of the country and its industrialisation. Doshi answered this question for himself by founding the Vastushilpa Foundation in 1956, with which he has since documented the traditional buildings in Ahmedabad through photographs, drawings and plans.

Identity, Attitude and Value

There are three topics that appear in Doshi's written work and characterise his architectonical thinking: namely identity, attitude and value. In his texts he approaches the buildings of the old city of Ahmedabad and its surroundings from the point of view of a professionally-trained architect. He describes the essential characteristics of buildings and shows the ways in which housing forms and structures react to environmental conditions, climate and geography. Economic and social conditions are also considered – Doshi attaches particular importance to customs, everyday life and religion. For him, building traditions must be

---

2 B. Doshi, 'Progetti in India tra urgenze contemporanee e tradizione', in *Spazio e Società*, no. 3, 1978, pp. 5–31.

3 V. S. Bader, 'The Vernacular is an Individualized Form of Architecture', in Mateo Kries, Khushnu Panthaki Hoof, Jolanthe Kugler (eds.), *Balkrishna Doshi: Architecture for the People,* Weil am Rhein, 2019, pp. 54–59.

respected and recognised as references. Only when the forms and technologies of building culture are understood can new approaches be found.[4] While lecturing in Japan in the 1960s, he found affirmation and inspiration from architects such as Kenzo Tange, Kiyonori Kikutake and Fumihiko Maki, who also dealt with the question of how a localised modernism could look. Through his analysis, Doshi ultimately determined the meaning of society's identity to be the confrontation of vernacular culture and building tradition. When he speaks of identity, he is concerned with an examination of these two different aspects.

For this reason, the loss of community in the cities has had a profound impact on him, which he also addresses in many of his writings. It is an expression of cultural attitude that he designs numerous public spaces and pieces of architecture. Unlike many of his colleagues, he has refused lucrative commissioned projects such as shopping centres and luxury condominiums throughout his long career. His focus is on communal, low-cost housing. Even when he designs homes, he sees the individual as part of the community. Doshi describes the house as the basis not only for private but also for public life. Here, the transitions are fluid, as inside and outside combine with both the urban fabric and the social context of the location. For this reason, he does not consider architecture as something isolated, but always in connection with respective urban and rural structures. Social life produces social space and the social space produces social life. It is this interweaving of architecture and life that interests Doshi – a basic attitude that defines his design. The architect 'should not just be a vehicle for the expression of different attitudes, but must be, through his skills and ingenuity, a builder of attitude as well.'[5]

Doshi exchanged ideas with Team X about the diverse relationships between public and private space. Its members, who came from the US, England, the Netherlands and Italy, had defied the dogma of the functional city and promoted a

---

4   B. Doshi, 'Identity in Architecture', in *Architectural Association Quarterly,* vol. 13, no. 1, October 1981, pp. 19–22.
5   B. Doshi, 'Toward an Appropriate Living Environment: Questions on Islamic Development', in Linda Safran (ed.), *Places of Public Gathering in Islam,* The Aga Khan Award for Architecture, 1980, pp. 135–137.

more human building practice, a 'human habitat'. In their designs they sought to integrate the many different needs of a pluralistic society. Foreign construction and ways of life became the starting point of their reflection. Aldo van Eyck wrote about the earth villages of the West African tribe of the Dogon, Alison and Peter Smithson, in their essay 'Collective Housing in Morocco', dealt with the Arabic courthouses, and in 1978, Giancarlo De Carlo edited the magazine *Spazio e Società,* in which authors devoted themselves to various concerns of the group. Doshi also published several essays here and thus joined the publishing activities of Team X.[6]

Unlike his colleagues in Europe and the United States, however, his interest in traditional building culture goes far beyond cultural and social factors. He extends his concept of architecture to the value of the spiritual, combined with rituals and ceremonies, which also includes the concept of timelessness. He finds likeminded people in the Iranian-born architect Nadar Adalan and the Egyptian Hassan Fathy. He met both at a conference in Tehran in 1976, where the manifesto *Habitat Bill of Rights* was written, to which Doshi contributed.[7] In the course of the discussions, these three architects insist that, despite industrialisation and new technologies, there should be a continuity in architectural design that empowers and supports people in their way of life. These are precisely the topics that interest Doshi: he is committed to an architecture in which these values are implicit, but also stands for self-determination and economic independence.

Creating Awareness and Reflection

The thoughts based on these experiences, which revolve around political, social and cultural conditions, have flowed into his written oeuvre. Since 1963 he has published about 40 essays in international specialist journals. He has also participated in numerous conferences in Japan, the US, Iran, Egypt, Switzerland,

---

6 A. Van Eyck, 'Architecture of the Dogon', in *Forum,* September 1961, pp. 116–21; A. Smithson, P. Smithson, 'Collective Housing in Morocco', in *Architectural Design,* January 1955, pp. 2–8; B. Doshi, 'Progetti in India tra urgenze contemporanee e tradizione', in *Spazio e Società,* no. 3, 1978, pp. 5–31. See also: V. S. Bader, 2019, p. 55.

7 N. Ardalan et al., *Habitat Bill of Rights,* Government of Iran, presented at the United Nations Conference on Human Settlements, Vancouver, 1976.

France, Finland and India. Today, at age 92, he continues to lecture and give interviews. In articles such as 'Identity in Architecture' (1981), 'Architecture and Attitudes' (1982) and 'Between Notion and Reality' (1989), key words like simplicity, adaptability, participation, cooperation, humility, dedication, stability and security emerge.[8] These core ideas determine his thought and action. Writing helps him become aware and reflect on his thoughts. A highlight here is certainly his own autobiography with the telling title *Path Uncharted,* which he published in 2011; 'uncharted' because his life has always led him to new unknown paths, but also because writing and drawing bring ideas to the surface.[9]

On the other hand his writings offer a theoretical foundation for his own architectural praxis. To a certain extent he employs the essence of what he has learned from his observations in order to define what he expects not only from himself, but from a modern Indian architectural vocabulary, too. Doshi's building projects invariably demonstrate his desire to unify architecture's diverse dimensions: he creates structures adapted to local landscapes and climate conditions (Gandhi Labour Institute, Ahmedabad, 1982). Instead of static solutions he designs ongoing processes that can accommodate or even demand changes (Aranya Low Cost Housing, Indore, 1989). In nearly all of his designs he experiments with open and closed spaces that in some instances allow for a variety of uses (Indian Institute of Management, Bangalore, 1977–92). Completely free of bias or dogma, Doshi creates richly diverse architectures that combine vernacular approaches with modern ideas allowing him to show how it is indeed possible to draw ever-new design ideas from this wealth of inspirations.[10] For this architecture, which embodies 'a sense of responsibility towards the people in this country', Doshi was finally awarded with the Pritzker Prize in March 2018.

8   B. Doshi, 'Identity in Architecture: Contemporary Pressures and Traditions in India', in *Architectural Association Quartely,* vol. 13, no. 1, October 1981, pp. 19–22; B. Doshi, 'Architecture and Attitudes', in *Akriti,* on the 24th Convention of National Association of Students of Architecture, 1982, pp. 4–6; B. Doshi, 'Between Notion and Realty', in *Contemporary Indian Tradition: Voices on Culture, Nature, and the Challenge of Change,* Washington D.C., Smithsonian Institution Press, 1989, pp. 335–353.
9   B. Doshi, *Paths Uncharted,* 2011.
10 V. S. Bader, 2019, p. 59.

INTERVIEW WITH BALKRISHNA DOSHI BY VERA SIMONE BADER

DATE: 10 MAY 2019
LOCATION: KAMALA HOUSE

What does writing mean to you?

First of all, writing comes almost automatically. I write the way the thoughts come, and so for me writing is understanding and clarifying my inner self. I have a lot of thoughts coming in and then through writing I realise that I already knew some of these thoughts and some of them I did not! So actually for me, writing is clarifying my inner thoughts.

Is there an interaction between writing and designing?

For me, writing helps immensely to understand the way space, form and structure manifest themselves. When I write, I begin to feel the dialogue, the movement and the kinds of stories they may have. But drawing actually comes from the kind of life that is going on inside of you, and when I draw I begin to see the superimposed nuances and I think about the moods that will happen in the space. For example, I see a column in a room and then the wall, so it is the eye that tells you about proportions, the eye that tells you about the sort of relationship they have and my own thoughts tell me about their conversation. So for me, writing and drawing belong together. Actually, I live my drawings and talk to my drawings through my writing.

Your texts are full of stories. What do they mean to you?

Actually stories are the kinds of dreams I have or the kinds of thoughts that I have only vaguely perceived and through which I begin to remember them. The stories are reminiscent of the gaps that happen in life. The most important thing for me is that when I look at things, I begin to feel a dialogue and the story behind it. This whole experience is like that of a theatre, but you are the visitor, the actor and you are also the creator. And in this creation, possibilities emerge, which in turn manifest through drawings. I can tell you why I say this: when I was working on the Mill Owners' Building in Paris, I had no idea how one should look at drawings and plans. So Corbusier picked up a drawing and he knew that things were not clear to me right away. So he took the coloured pencils and drew a line, 'You see, there is a wall.' And then he drew a column and said, 'Now we want to make a theatre but where are the people? They come out of the elevator and they are moving through the room, they would turn and walk around and then the podium is here and the visitors are sitting there.' He would describe it in this way to me. So this was my first lesson in life! This drawing, the spaces, the connotation and calligraphy of the drawing and the movement, they all go together to form architecture.

So what's architecture in this context?

It is not just architecture! It is an experience, it is a narration, it is a thought. The main idea is that I really look at everything as if it is a living organism. For example, for me this column is not just a column and for this wall that runs along and turns around, I think, the wall wants to stand a little further away from the column, and then when I bring it closer and closer, the dialogue begins to happen! Because each has its own inert life that we do not know about and that we have to discover.

You also mention a lot of myths in your texts. How do they connect to you?

They are part of my life, absolutely! Because I know them from my childhood. Most of the time, the problems come up when we start to condition children. We tell them the meaning of things. It is an absolutely cold, clear-cut thing, like the way I'm sitting on this chair and you're sitting there. But for me, life is a theatre, because I sense the dialogue and that dialogue is my dialogue. It may not be a real dialogue. It is rather that I make conjectures from the kinds of things I am doing so the myth is already there. Myth is always prevalent in my work. Myth is a story that helps to create the character of space and when that character emerges, there is a footprint of that myth, and in this footprint you can find subtle nuances.

You wrote once that good design must include several tangible and intangible things. Where exactly do you find them in your architecture?

This is what you find in my architecture, yes. Because tangible is a diagram but the intangible is the way the diagram is expressed. It is the location between that space where the dialogue can happen, so space becomes a very active thing. It is like in a book with different players and these players are having the dialogue.

So what do you feel or think about vernacular architecture? You had already begun to write about this topic in the sixties at the same time when Bernard Rudofsky put on his famous exhibition Architecture Without Architects *at the MoMA.*

I met Bernard Rudofsky in Japan and we became good friends. He also came here to Ahmedabad, when I opened the office. The amazing thing was that he naturally wore a kimono in Japan and lived in a Japanese room. He had many photos and all the photos showed the *shōji,* doors and everything else, but with cracks and paper ribbons. I said, 'Bernard why? What are you doing?' He said, 'You know, I like that fragility.' They were all collaged, everything had tape and the various tapes became a pattern and these patterns became something else. Perhaps it was a Zen thing because he lived that way and he looked at the whole idea of putting things together with tape. So there were fragments and then there were connections and then there were stories, because one would ask, 'Is it connected in this way?' The question that we are not asking nowadays is how architects reinterpret space, form and structure. There are so many ways. So this is how I knew Bernard Rudofsky.

And did you meet Giancarlo De Carlo also?

Yes, of course I met him.

What was your common topic?

Our common topic was life. For example, we talked about the studio and then we had dinner or maybe walked through an old city centre in Italy, say Siena or some other place. Or he showed me the building that he was doing. We talked about space. We talked about movement. The spaces became alive through our conversation and we were interested in how many ways space could tell us a story. Our questions were about the various ways spaces, forms, volumes, structures, characters and climate could affect the people's psyche, and I think this is important! We never looked at the people's psyche and asked how it would be affected over time. However, we were interested in the indirect moods that a space creates, and indeed this is the place where myth or dialogue can take place.

Then what do you think about tropical modernism?

For me it is dead [laughing]. It's strange because as you ask, childhood comes into play. For example, when I walked in the streets then I saw the different balconies. People were standing there. Sometimes they put clothes on the balcony and sometimes I saw children there. I began to see how many ways spaces are used, formally-informally – but they become alive. It's like human beings. You dress up for different occasions and you accept that. But in modernism a balcony is a balcony and you only have a certain position from which to stand and look out. It is not anything else. It doesn't go beyond! That is why I don't like the idea of modernism. Modernism relates to function. There is already a theory that has specified everything... life is not like this! Our Indian food, you cannot specify it, because we have things that change your taste. And, where is participation? I think that is the question! It is important that the user has the chance to participate and discover his inner ideas or thoughts that he never considered before. So is he awakened? Can he awaken himself? And then, would he get attached to it? I think it is very important for architects to create their own awakening. Otherwise, one doesn't receive the ownership. This is what I think.

I read that you participated at the CIAM meeting in 1951. Did the topic 'The Heart of the City' affect you?

Well, at that time I was not old enough to understand the whole picture of what I was doing. At the congress, they said that people were thinking more and more about the city centre and were talking about how people gather and meet. From this point of view, I was very happy to talk about people and society and their activities and relationships. But it did not go beyond that. What I am talking about today goes way beyond.

Yes, sure. But at that time you also experienced postwar Europe. Did the post-catastrophic situation influence you?

I was in Europe after the war in the 1950s. What surprised me was the passion with which they reconstructed. For me, it was like recreating the world they knew, as well as building a world they imagined and would like to have. I think that is something I remember: they built homes, they built spaces and then they talked about the future – about the world of tomorrow. They were interested in mobility and relationships.

I once had a meeting with James Stirling. Giancarlo De Carlo was also there, and Aldo van Eyck. I was there and we talked about these issues and then they asked me, 'What are you doing?' So, I said that 'I am doing some housing.' I started to show them the housing, even the houses of the old city of Ahmedabad and what I had done. Mine was very structured, while the townhouses had balconies and other things. So they said, 'But how come? What do you think about these?' In another meeting, Charles Eames asked me an important question: 'You show us Udaipur and other things, but they are quite different from what you are doing! There are balconies, there are projections, there are *chhajjas* and not in your buildings!' And this was the first time I realised that what he asked was right.

The questions that I was looking at were how they handled traditions in their work and then, of course, how they could be reconstructed with new technology?

And it was important then to talk about the society or the street. So what happened was we began to ask what kind of life we would lead. I think those kinds of questions are very important. My understanding of architecture is time, tolerance, identity and continuity. And I started to elaborate on this topic. At this point I had various questions such as those about time and who are you? What are you? What are your needs and does it relate to your needs? Will you get the identity that is yours? And indeed, this conference of the fifties might have helped me to look directly at Aranya, my low-cost housing project. In Aranya I began to ask myself questions: How do you identify a place that is not designed by yourself? And if the habitants want to change something, will they not be able to expand or add anything? Isn't it normal that they should want to change their life in the way they want it? And isn't it normal that they continue and add something more? In Aranya, I saw the kinds of spaces that have transformed and that have been added to with different passages. They were very narrow, but life has improved there. Well when I started to experience this, I thought that technically and legally it may not be right. But for their social, cultural and economic needs, this is appropriate and my aesthetic attitude began to change.

What changes do you permit to your own buildings?

It depends on the purpose, scale, character and typology of the project as well as who makes the changes. But there are certainly examples like the LIC housing, where I allowed changes for the first time. I saw that the habitants added some colour. I had previously given different colours, but they changed them. So I started to change my mind about it, in the sense that I have no right to judge them aesthetically or to call their other choices right or wrong. Of course, sometimes I am saddened to think that the changes they make do not work very well. But when I ask them, they say that they are very happy. So I wonder what the role of an architect really is? Am I only a social anthropologist or a technical person if I cannot talk about aesthetics? But ultimately the question is not correct. If they feel very happy and want to change their home, then I should not rethink my own ideas. I know that the changes can be very chaotic. Sometime things become terrible. But who knows. As I'm growing older and older I know that things are changing in life. Who wants to carry the old baggage and make the judgement?

I have to ask you one comprehensive question. Yesterday I visited the museum of Le Corbusier in Ahmedabad. I was very touched when I saw this building die. And inside there is this exhibition about the city. Can you explain why this building does not work?

Actually, there are different things. I was in Ahmedabad to finish Corbusier's museum and when it was finished I was fascinated by the beauty. People asked, 'What will come into this box?' Then I planted ivy on the gutter – which is still there, but now broken. Green creepers should hang on the wall like a green cover. On the roof hydroponics such as tomatoes and others should be grown. This was the beginning, six or eight months after the building was finished. When it was under construction, people came and saw that this box was slowly being covered with brick walls. They were pretty shocked because they did not know what was happening inside. When I saw the empty space with the columns, I felt that this is another world apart from the old city. The old city is a community – private, small-scale. Everything is like this. But this is a public building and a new way of talking about culture – a new way of thinking about exhibitions, ideas, the future and diversion. But the expression was very different from the old buildings. Of course that means change – radical change in the concept of traditional or vernacular architecture. Sometimes you have to leave the old for completely new ideas: like the museum raised from the ground with a little courtyard. There is a pond and there are some fish and water and some reflections. I think all those things were another world to me and I was very happy that this building would eventually grow and things would happen there so that people could understand that you cannot compare different kinds of spaces, relationships and activities, such as when you have old houses, an old city and then a big palace, or a large temple complex. They are different because the scale is different. This message is

important. That is why I liked the design and did not put it together for comparison. For me, there was no comparison between what small- and large-scale are! And of course today I am very dissatisfied with what happens!

And the display?

The display is actually a small replica of the city. The plan was to show Ahmedabad as a living city. In this vibrant city you can see corners where different religions are practised, different festivals take place and different kinds of activities are pursued. We thought of having guides that the visitors could take with them. Then they would take a rickshaw that would take them to the place where printing, crafts, architecture and different behaviours or religions are demonstrated. That was what was really meant for this building. It should be a cultural centre. It is actually known in Gujarati as the so-called cultural centre 'Sanskar Kendra'.

And why did this not work?

Because it became a warehouse. A warehouse in the sense that things from different places were put together. This is the end. But the intention was to establish a cultural centre that proliferates and demonstrates what is happening outside. There should be an interaction with the visitors. It was thought of like this! But there was never participation. In Ahmedabad, holidays comprise 20% of the year. We have different festivals of different religions. Some religions have a very small number of believers and others are much larger. All of them are participatory. Similarly there were craft centres that were useful for the religion. So there was a sociocultural integration into what people do and what they produce. This was really very important, because where do you find a living city with such coexisting diversity and everybody participating. Second, there were people who were part of the city and who contributed to the city's development. The third part was the production. For the museum, the idea never matured. It was never realised. But if done properly, I am sure the museum would have been the model for how the city functions. That did not happen. In other words, it is sustainable to architecturally create a cultural centre based on participation. It should give the talents, beliefs and skills that exist in the city a chance to go beyond themselves. All of these things did not happen and that's why the museum almost died. Because people will not come to a place that is not bound to their religions, their behaviours or their skills. And if I don't invite them to come, then no one will come. It will not work. Still, it was a very good building. I think it was very well done with the most beautiful proportions. When it was drawn, Ernesto Rogers was in the office and he looked at the facade with the proportions and he said to Le Corbusier, 'Monsieur, does it not look like it was drawn by Leonardo?'

Once I curated an exhibition about Lina Bo Bardi. She also had the idea to exhibit the art and crafts of ordinary people in Salvador. In Brazil she was the first who was really interested in these kinds of cultural objects and she integrated the people of the city into the institution. Can you compare her concept with your ideas?

Yes, she was very much interested in such things. I looked at myself and asked, 'Who am I? What do I do? Does it really have value and meaning? And if I dab a small stone and drop it into the water, would the way it touches the periphery create a broader horizon, a larger understanding?' When Corbusier's buildings were built, the most important thing began to happen. In the sixties, various institutions in Ahmedabad such as the Institute of Management of Louis Kahn, the National Institute of Design of Gira Sarabhai and other institutions emerged. I also did the School of Architecture. The whole idea was that when we really have this fellowship, then we start to talk about art, crafts, music, theatre etc, and not just that. If we use these open spaces, then we start to activate the whole city. This is important, because everywhere you go there is a mixed population. At least that was how it was. It was the beauty of the old city. They had a variety of activities there. In the real old city everything was mixed up: informal-formal, different disciplines, co-operation, sharing, economic ways of movement, transformed network, everything was connected and you did not even have a notion of time. Like people who are shopkeepers. They tend to live above their shops. If somebody needed something at night, the lady or someone would come down and give it to you. That means you had constant activity and a constant mix. In the old part of the town, temples, schools and washing areas, all coexisted. All those things were unique in the city and I think that's because there is energy. And if you come in contact with it through different kinds of unusual activities, you increase wealth and pull energy. We really should start doing these kinds of things together with the city plan. When the School of Architecture started along with other institutions – there was also a very good theatre with excellent music programmes – things were really active. If this had really continued, we would have a very different kind of city with the basic idea of mixing and connecting. I think that's one of the most important things to consider in today's plans. We should talk about the different displays and possibilities in the cities and about extensions rather than talking about bringing cities or clusters together. That really fascinated me and that's why the School of Architecture had all the different disciplines. We even have a visual art centre there. We taught fine arts, visual art and we had a theatre and music. The campus was comprised of all these things. And I think the role of an architect is to incorporate such diversity.

Did you have contact with the other Indian architects of your generation? How did they think about these ideas?

I had connections, yes. We were very close friends. I met everyone immediately after the Independence. Let's say from 1955 to 1960 – those were the times when the institutes came into existence. The architectural schools started in Delhi, then Calcutta, then Chennai. They were a couple of years old. We all dealt with cultural connections, cultural history and the meaningful attitude to life and work. Everyone was thrilled when we met, but we never met all together. The country is too big. We were busy with our own local area. The climate is different, the economic levels and also the client requirements are different. It's not a small country, you know! We talked about it, but we never went beyond it. We never started something like the Indian Institute of Architects or the Council of Architecture. Everyone was busy! Look, if you are young, if you have ideas and want to start your career, then you are quite busy. So, there was no centre, no traditional institution that emerged.

Today we have 600 schools of architecture, and if we found just one connection, one headquarters or a main institution, then everything would be fine! We don't have to agree on one idea but I miss a consciousness for a larger context. We need to be aware in India of what needs to be done today, what is meaningful and useful for society as a whole. Because we have big differences: we have villages, we have slums, we have towns and we have megacities. I think a new kind of communication could make us much more active. It's not about a big university but a centre where we often come together and talk about it. I think everyone is looking for it, because the world is changing rapidly – even the architecture profession. Everyone questions its relevance. Take a look at the kinds of conferences and trips that are taking place. Everything expands, but everything dissolves.

So you want to bring the things together?

Mobility is there. Huge mobility and opportunities and different ideas are there, but who is going to bring them together? Conferences are just as relevant as exhibitions if there is a dialogue. But it is necessary to pass this dialogue on to other places and discuss it. For example, why does the Biennale not spread from Venice? Such things could happen and they could be very useful.

And I think that the role of the museum now is also relevant in this respect. Because it is a centre of culture – a centre of new ideas and thoughts. If museums from different parts of the world organise meetings and then disseminate their discussions through publications, this would be very good for everyone. I think that in this way, the museum could be an even more dynamic place.

INTERVIEW WITH BALKRISHNA DOSHI

If you had the chance to build whatever you wanted in Ahmedabad, what would it be?

I wish that the Bhadra Plaza would be frequented as a city centre. It was one of the first that was established in Ahmedabad. In the immediate vicinity there is a fortress, a temple, mosques, a bazaar and other shops. In this place you can get an idea of what the city is about. But unfortunately it did not materialise as planned. So if I had the chance, then I would connect the Bhadra Plaza with any open space in the peripheries or in the centre and establish a relationship so that the city in these places could really start to pulsate, creating relationships and opportunities that go beyond what people normally do – so the Bhadra Plaza would be a part of the world today.

Thank you!

REGIONALITY

1960

Change is a basic universal law.

The human need is to grasp what it considers to be permanent. 'Permanence changes', says Kant.
'Permanence which gives up an old form and assumes a new form is real', says the Jain view of reality.

The recognition that any set of conditions may provoke more than satisfying solutions is the basis of change and continuing creativity. The architect's task is to study and understand the traditions of a people within a region and to study as well the forces and in some cases to force certain changes in the life of the people by his knowledge of a healthy and refined life.

Regionality is the culture of a people living in a particular area with certain specific qualities of their own. This element is apparent in the history of all art forms in the East and the West. With the gradual expansion of communication, the accumulation of great heritages of different communities and the spread of their influences in the surrounding area are also observed through their folk, domestic and monumental art forms.

Limited communications and limited observations resulted in localisation of expression in the past. Rapid technological and scientific developments led to a total rejection of age old ways substituting in their place a rootless expression of more industrial functionalism with a view to explore new possibilities. This has given us art and architecture more or less uniform throughout the world. The non-affective and materialist expression over the last few decades has awakened many people, who feel uprooted and are trying to understand the cause and reason for abandoning ideas of the past.

The thirst for change not being fully satisfied has again bounced with greater force and today we are faced with multiple questions in our confused mind as to what should be done to express the location and the existence of our roots – which was so long done and appreciated in the past. Our task today, therefore, would be to analyse the problem, the reason, the place of our heritage, the cause of the previous continuity and the factors which contributed to the satisfying evolution of the past centuries which have not been taken into account in the recent times.

By basing the analysis on the abstract values, one finds that the following conditions affected and marked the tradition of a place or of a region. The likes and dislikes were also gradually evolved due to the same.

Climate
Geography
Flora and fauna
Language
Costume and food production
Social habits and patterns of life
Dwellings and household equipment
Communication and spiritual urge

A group of people without any bias going from nowhere to a place would slowly try to adjust themselves to the climate and the geography. The crops and the food that they would produce will be determined by the first two factors and then by adjustments, they would decide their routine of work. This pattern in turn will then define to a certain extent their social customs, habits and their dwellings or the way of living. Simultaneously through the experience of geography and other factors, language, music, poetry and literature will evolve. As long as they are isolated, their evolution will entirely depend on the ingenuity and aspirations of this group of people. The change in economy will also be affected by their attitude on life based on the climate and geography.

However, the basic change would be first felt when the established communication is changed, ie the contacts are enlarged and more exchanges take place. The economic change due to the communication would further modify the

techniques of productions verified through the material advantage. This will then modify their so far established social pattern, customs, the equipment in the dwellings and the dwellings themselves. But surprisingly the added communication will not succeed fast in influencing the climate, geography, flora and fauna. The language and more so the mental and the emotional attitude towards the objects of their feelings would be even more difficult to change fast.

In these difficult to change attitudes one finds certain peculiar characteristics always mentioned as regional.

Now what are these traits that are then defined as 'regional'? In our everyday observations, when we use the world regional, it expresses two different meanings – good and bad, fresh and narrow, appreciative and non-appreciative, expression that is specific and not in general routine and an expression or an attitude which has resulted from a limited knowledge and from the refusal of any change. Nevertheless developed communication makes us aware that there could be several solutions to a given problem when looked at from various angles and if consciously explored, the advantages would not only be the acceptance of other attitudes but also the awareness of our own qualities, and defects. It would also create a rich climate of stimulation.

The wider contacts and the present education has developed our consciousness to a considerably higher level in order to enable us to self-consciously analyse the traditions, their good and bad qualities and to reject or absorb the new qualities seen and felt. The people who immediately influence the region through outside communications are the elites – educationists, social workers, designers and architects and artists. And hence change may be immediately accepted by them but will not be accepted by the larger group.

Therefore, it is of utmost importance that we try to clearly state the set of values which should lead towards a complete and wholesome fulfillment of life. At various stages of life, a continuously variable but constantly harmonious relationship of the material and the spiritual values formulate wholesome needs which are properly fulfilled by the good object. The gradual evolution of the good object was a non-personal process within the total understanding of the available technology. The good object being made for a specific and clearly defined use expressed a significance which was universally understood. The good object created with humility and in profound respect of the highest values acquired a straightforward nobility and brought dignity and enrichment to the life of the times and became an expression of he prevailing culture.

However, given the choice, the preferences and evaluation would be mostly based on the values impressed upon the individual or the group through the conditioning of tradition and education.

The creative mind always succeeds in adopting the most diverse elements to the immediacy of the local circumstances. This process whether conscious or not is clearly a recognition of the natural significance of regionality.

'Let culture flow……….' …… Gandhi.

To illustrate: Architecture is conditioned by the culture of a people. Culture is social heritage which at a particular moment of time will be confined to a particular geographical region. But the social heritage is not necessarily conditioned by present day environments. It may have many vestiges of other regional environments – the sum total of social heritage in a particular region might have to include factors natural to other regions. When an architect builds for a particular region, he has to take into consideration the needs and the expectations formed by these various factors. Eg Fatehpur Sikri (sarcenic expectations plus geographical conditions). The general stylistic approach came from outside India but all that was completely accepted and very carefully and completely matched to the conditions of that time. And this resulted in an expression which is quite different from what happened in the place of origin at this time, ie sarcenic architecture becoming Indianised.

Conclusion:
The human condition of change is not basically a series of rejections, but rather an oscillating sequence of creative reactions to aspects of the past and of unprecedented situations. In a long perspective of time, change is confrontation of the heritage through a continuing accumulation of new experience.

In this way heritage is modified, furthered and continued.

INDIAN ARCHITECTURE AND ITS CRITICISM

1965

Criticism helps us understand the stage of development of a culture as well as its components. It is well known that art is such an essential element in every culture. In fact Malinowski regards art as one of the cultural imperatives along with knowledge or science, religion and magic.

Social heritage is the key concept of culture according to the same authority.
1. This applies pari passu to art as well. Art therefore must be studied as an integral part of social heritage.

Architecture in European tradition is one of the major fine arts along with sculpture and painting, and music and poetry. Historically considered, architecture, sculpture and painting have grown together. In fact in the early stages of every culture, sculpture and painting were more or less decorative elements or architecture. Thus historically architecture is basic, finding in itself place for sculpture and painting. Herbert Spencer pointed out long ago that it was in the course of time that sculpture and painting became independent arts, exciting in their own right.
2. This inter-existence is no where better illustrated than in the ancient architecture of India.

In order to discover the norms by which we would judge Indian architecture we must study it as social heritage. As we know from history, architecture – the art of enclosures – is seen in its efficiently developed form as early as the Harappan culture (c2500 BC). Even though we have not been fortunate to discover architectural remains between this age and Mauryan times (c400 BC) we would not be wrong if we assume that architectural tradition in India is nearly 5,000 years old. If one studies the archaeological remains to architecture along with the work on *Vastu Shastra* one would find that there is an elaborate and systematic knowledge about various kinds of architecture, starting from the layout of villages, towns, cities and forts as well as precise rules about building houses for gods, kings and ordinary mortals.
3. As is to be expected the Vastu of ancient India was intimately related to other aspects of its culture.

This long history and tradition, however, received a rude shock and was set back under the British domination. Indian architecture was a living tradition even in Moslem times. It had even then vitality to absorb West-Asian influences and yet remain characteristically Indian. This, however, could not continue under the economic pressure of the British rulers. It ultimately ended in the destruction of arts and crafts of India. Architecture was no exception.

Thus in the long architectural tradition of India, a gap has occurred. What we have had as architecture under the British rule is a sort of hybrid thing which does not possess the great qualities of either Indian or European architecture. In fact one could not help saying that there is nothing like Indian architecture in modern times, excepting a few temples being built here and there by some traditional master craftsmen.

Under the circumstances, the task of a critic of Indian architecture of modern times is much more difficult and different from that of critics of architecture in other countries; because Indian architectural tradition was not allowed the chance which architectural traditions of other countries had and which it had in the pre-British period of this country. We for this very reason, find painful differences when the Indian architecture of the present day is compared with these of the West. Hence the task of the critic of architecture in India would be different. It would be to find out as to how this hiatus can be removed, how old architectural values of Indian culture can be brought to light and examined with the aid of modern developments in science and technology.

Criticism of Indian architecture therefore will have to concern itself with understanding how social heritage is modifying itself in our present conditions and how architecture would become an integral part of it, because architecture is an art which organises, coordinates and orders life by its function of providing enclosure to beings for their wholesome needs.

July 78

The true Indian architecture that is to be born will have its norms as an art of utility through its function and as an art of beauty through its appeal to the inherited aesthetic sensibility of an Indian.

In the West architectural development has occurred with continuity and any change has been a source of practical observation, application and judgement resulting in a suitable form of the time. The living tradition of architecture in the West is becoming up-to-date during the past few decades with respect to science and technology and is broadening and humanising itself not in romantic reaction but through the natural progress of scientific thought. The contemporary architecture therefore recognises that man has dignity, personality, spiritual meaning and realises that it is inseparable from the social setting and hence from architecture. The same would be in accordance with the Indian tradition.

Criticism in order to be useful would have to be based on historical and traditional knowledge as well as empirical and experimental. It should approve or condemn concrete examples on the basis of tested facts. In order to make its interpretation sensible and effective it must demonstrate how a piece of architecture is an integral part of the living culture in its different aspects such as religious, social, political-economical, physical-psychological on one side and scientific, technical, spatial and functional on the other.

If today we have to create enthusiasm for architecture, it will be necessary to educate the architects and the public in this new orientation which is really vital because it has its roots in the consciousness of the people and because it will have utilised the results of modern progress in architectural science and art. In this way, with a proper historical and cultural approach in education and practice, it would not be far long when we too shall become aware of our problems in architecture and find solutions for them of which we can talk, discuss and be proud.

RURAL HOUSING

1970

Village street – end
shaded porches, outdoor
living spaces, open to sky
sleeping.

June 83

All cultural or historical studies base their primary interpretations about the general activity on the findings of the then existing physical environment. This procedure is followed since all activities and the physical environment behave as counterparts. As and when activity modifies or accelerates, changes in the physical environment become inevitable. If not accepted, friction and conflict between activity and physical environment takes place and ultimately reduce the potency of the anticipated result.

This implies that for a community to develop in harmony it is essential to balance the activity with the environment.

Our present urban scene shows this kind of conflict since the pace of change between the physical environment and our activities is different. With the result we in cities are not at ease with our surroundings. We continuously struggle between our need to find a congenial place to live, to educate our children or to go to a nearby place of work. This has happened due to many reasons but to my mind it's our lack of understanding of function and its relation to the physical form. For example houses which we see today in the cities do not come anywhere near to our daily needs as either an individual or a family.

These houses as you will notice are built as series of rooms without any regard to a specific function. Simple factors such as proper ventilation or temperature control lack in these so-called houses. As a group these houses do not even depict any kind of community life which is expected of any housing.

Perhaps all this is due to our notion that people in the cities are on the move and they are a 'faceless' mass.

Our rural areas which today look so congenial and peaceful will very soon change their static garb and will slowly follow the speedy path of our urban life. With the green revolution, mechanisation, electrification and improved communication villages will no more remain the same. The land price, the cost of building materials will rise beyond our scope and we will then adopt the same procedure as that of the cities and end up with the same frustrations of a city life mentioned earlier.

But, it's quite possible that we can follow another path suitable to the situation if we think from right now. We can retain in the process of change most of the qualities of the existing rural areas which we cherish so much and at the same time follow the advantageous methods of the urban world.

For example, in most of the villages the principal place of activity is the community place. Every other activity including housing is planned around this place and all activities are interwoven as one single fabric of life. It is very apparent when we visit a village or see a village plan how important a *chowk,* or a *chabutra,* a well or a temple is. These elements seem to belong to the village as much as the houses. There is no indication of their being planned in isolation.

The houses in which people live and which form a major bulk of the village are function oriented and are not designed as 'cells' that are seen in the cities.

These houses are planned to suit the needs of the occupant and even their location is related to the inhabitants, occupation and place of work. For example, a house of a farmer with his cattleshed and fodder storage, a house of a merchant with his shop and its storage, a well adjoining, a community, platform in the crucial location are indications of a rural scene and a rural life. This basic relationship between the function and the form and climate has direct bearing upon the people and as a result we feel a certain amount of harmony in a village.

This implies that if we consider these points and plan, our changing rural areas will still have the hope of achieving something more than the urban areas without sacrificing any of the new technological advantages.

To illustrate this idea of foresighted planning, let me take an example of a house, and the needs of the user. Housing to be effective must allow a certain amount of flexibility to suit functional needs, give some scope for future additions and changes as and when needs modify, and, in addition, to transform the house according to his choice to call it his 'own' so that he can identify the same from others and associate with it all his life. As said earlier, the rural mud or brick house somehow is able to satisfy these needs.

These necessities, if not foreseen, and provided for in the overall plan, will not be realised afterwards due to economic pressures and resources. But in fact advanced changing technology should be able to do this with greater ease. This can be done by providing initially the basic services in an overall plan and gradually providing a place for a kitchen and a bathroom to ensure hygiene. The open space that will be left around this can become for the time being temporary living quarters with ideally separation between the cattle and the human beings. With increase in economic resources the inhabitant then can build around this service core a room, or services of rooms in either mud, brick or in prefabricated panels to ensure shelter, protection, privacy etc. This procedure will have the scope to change all along gradually ensuring greater comforts which the user would aspire to in course of time. All these changes will then encourage more identification with the surroundings, greater exploitation of the available resources and a naturally better life. It can be also made possible to provide for vertical expansion when the land is limited.

And, all this can happen with the participation of the community. The community can develop schemes for built-in resources in building housing and community facilities together. Community will then become the pivot of the rural housing and it will have once again a central place in the master plan.

As a device, to ensure this concept we can reorganise our existing village or plan our new village with a provision for the two kinds of elements – one which is capable of changing at smaller scales, say a house or components of a house at the demands of scales, an individual and the other at communal scale, which is more permanent and only changes when a radical change is required. This way, we will be able to succeed in achieving our goals of creating environments which will become counterpart to our activities.

This kind of mutual interdependence will allow the so much needed initiative within the individual and harmony within the total village. This will then save our so much wasted natural resources such as rain water, sewage effluents waste, land and make the village a good deal self-sufficient.

Once this is begun, the chain reaction of using our latent potential will gradually filter into other areas and due to sheer necessity and demand open new avenues for small-scale industries for housing components required at many places. Housing then will not remain a mere isolated element but will become an active occupation leading to the creation of better personalised or localised houses as in the past.

It's then quite likely that this kind of attempt will influence to reduce the apathy shown towards urban housing; and once again all housing irrespective of a simple unit, or a cluster, or an extension to a city will blossom as a place to nourish, grow and live together.

VALUES AND SCALES. MUSINGS OF AN ARCHITECT

1974

The problem of the role of architecture and urban planning in industrialising countries has assumed prominence at a time when the world is at crossroads. There are nations overindustrialised and worried about decreasing resources and greater ecological disasters. On the other hand there are countries which are just awakening from their so-called slumber and have looked through TV 'how backward we are economically' and so they want to industrialise – come what may! And in between there are countries which are on their way to industrialisation but do not know what direction to take.

These disturbing conditions, strange enough, have one problem in common – Man and his environment, his working conditions, how his surroundings can provide opportunities for leisure after a long hard working day. These are the factors that every planner and architect should think of.

An architect and a planner who is involved in one or other of these stages of development is facing a dilemma. He does not know what direction to take. Though his main goal is to plan for a comfortable, happy and peaceful life, his efforts are thwarted. The reasons are very simple. He cannot solve either the economic or political problems of his country. He has to willy-nilly, accept whatever social, political or economic situations that have arisen, and find a short term remedial solution in either planning or architecture or both.

This too has to be within limitations. He, somehow, attempts to provide for maximum comfort, peace and leisure to the individual, to the family and to the community as a whole. Though this is his priority, he is like a carriage whose driver he is not. Therefore he neither can take initiative, nor control it, much less guide it. The control is with the main decision-makers – the man or men with the reins. All of us in this profession know this.

As a consequence, our profession has accepted that our planning and architecture have to be for a short-term future, say a year or at the most a few years. But a decade is too long. Not having any base for long-lasting solutions and in absence of any specific goal, our architectural and planning solutions follow naturally the styles in vogue. They look to immediacy and unfortunately justify their creation. Theories based on these solutions are developed and then changed when a new idea crops up. This constant change in expression and purpose goes on unabated.

Our present professional world, its pursuit and the work clearly indicate this state of affairs.

And this is happening everywhere: in industrialised and industrialising countries as well as the ones which are thinking of industrialising. And again, unfortunately, the styles in architecture and planning pursued by the developed countries are limited by the developing countries without adequate thought. The pattern of change is due to the notion that all problems of development in the world are basically connected with economic affluence and hence they should be persuaded with a view to achieve economic affluence.

We have begun to believe that the destiny of all humanity is already chartered and the path taken by the industrialised world – namely that of economic affluence – is the path to be taken without further consideration. Whether this has relevance to our concept of life and other goals or not, the already tracked path is accepted in toto.

As said earlier, not having control over economic and political affairs, our planning and architectural solutions have to start on and follow the same path.

The results are naturally incongruous because our conditions and need do not demand the same solution nor the same pattern as offered by developed countries.

It is said, 'Every culture has just the future that is contained in the dynamic force of its image of the future. The future of a culture can be predicted by the power of its thinking about the future. No culture can maintain itself for long without a positive and generally accepted image of the future. A culture which shuts itself up in the present or what amounts to the same thing, in a short-sighted perspective of the future, has no future.' This quotation taken from Mr Berteaux's book, *The Future,* means that before beginning the march towards future, and to achieve the desired results, we must build an image of our choice – in the perspective of our needs and capacities.

Even though the rulers may be aware that their main aim is to provide, while industrialising, people's basic needs – food, shelter, work and comfort if possible. By following the pattern laid down by the industrialising nations, they can achieve quicker results through short-circuiting the process. No doubt, this is possible and may be wanted, but here also the effort is being based on wrong premises. It does not relate to our own tradition, culture and socio-economic needs. Hence the relationship between means and ends does not match. The anxiety to develop faster and to elevate the people's lot in the shortest possible time results into undesirable situations. Unfortunately at a great cost.

With mounting internal and external pressures to fulfil the promises with disregard for the political and social institutions and without the know-how in technology, the aspiring countries succumb to these conditions. In addition, the 'generous' affluent world market with its promise of technological assistance and the mass media with 'the message' arrive at their doorstep. The excited population gathers momentum without any consideration of the goals of life and compels the leaders to accept the development plan. Industrialisation and urbanisation should take place in the country to the true welfare of the people.

Unfortunately, the impact of such acceptance appears rather late. The changes begin to affect the working method and lifestyles of the people. The imported technologies do not match with the know-how or the habits of the people at the right wave length and disharmony sets in. Things somehow do not work as efficiently as anticipated. Since there is no plan prepared for this change and transition, the mistake continues. There is a fear of our own condemnation and the world pressure. The clock does not turn back. To add to this chaos, in the developing countries (without proper education) population continues to grow and migration to urban areas takes place. Uncoordinated planning and underuse as well as misuse of technology create unexpected difficult situations.

The present architecture and urban planning without any roots, faith or image takes its own form expressing the above-mentioned state of affairs.

In such situations, what kind of role can we expect from architecture and urban planning? Since the entire development has depended on uncontrolled circumstances and has discounted 'Man' for whom it was meant, what style of buildings can we expect? What kind of plan do we expect? What can be taught in the schools? What professional services can we offer?

Where do we really begin?

The effects of such uncoordinated development has more disastrous effects in industrialising and developing countries than in the industrialised countries. For where can the poor nations find additional resources to rectify its ever-growing mistakes of blind imitation?

Besides, the cultural shock is even greater. It questions even the basis of earlier lifestyles, the value of architecture and the city planning of the past. The conflict between the old which was one's own and the new but alien, and apparently impressive, aggravates. Happiness, which should be a continuing process, discontinues and is no more available.

For example, India with her over half a million villages with about 580 million population, and with her agricultural economy, is facing the problem of food shortage today. This has occurred because our emphasis until a few years ago was on heavy industry and not on simultaneously developing small and cottage industries. As a result, we have today extreme stages of development without proper

links. We have sophisticated technology including the atomic power plants and jet air transportation in some areas and bullock carts in some others. The few cities are getting overpopulated with industries concentrated in them and the smaller towns and villages getting deserted due to shortages of even basic needs. In such unexpected and unbalanced development what could be the so-called priorities of architecture? At which end of the stick should we begin?

This state of things once it begins is difficult to control. For in such a situation the technologies of creating material for basic needs are in great demand. The mass media-radio-television-films have brought to the mostly uneducated population an area of awareness in the lifestyle of developed countries. As a consequence, the fast growing population on a limited developed land mass, has built an aspiration of a new world – a world of health and comfort. New gadgets that are seen through the mass media become a fascination. The choice with them is to search for a place where the happiness of their dream can be found. The reaction naturally is to move – to a better place. Thus movement from less developed to developed places takes place. No one is able to control this exodus from rural to urban areas.

This pattern is not peculiar to India only: it is happening all over the industrialising countries.

We note that this situation is unavoidable as a consequence of industrialisation. But then what solutions have we for either the urban or the rural areas? Since the technological benefits should be given to the masses, irrespective of their location, what are we, as architects and planners, doing? Are we really developing a technology for either better living conditions or directing through education and planning some ways of helping the rural population to have a better shelter or well-planned industry for lean periods or better tools for farming?

Let us see – how is nature with its innumerable varieties still able to not only sustain itself but make things grow and continue in their adjusted and interdependent cycles? What kind of logic does nature have? How does it manage and with what kind of managerial skills does it respond to a particular situation? And, how does it make a variety of elements live together? And above all how does it control various timescales, in life spans or other temporal cycles? For example, if nature had decided that there will be no limit to growth, imagine what will be the consequences? An animal will grow and grow, and grow so much that it will not like to have a rival and get crushed under its own weight. In such a world of giants there will be fewer species of animals and plants. This would result in a loss of variety. There might be hugeness but probably extinction also. This does not require an explanation. But nature is wise enough not to do this. The logic of nature lies in proper relation of the function and form. It does not tend to create merely huge corpulent entities like we tend to do in our planning.

Hence, in terms of operation and management for balanced growth, we need to discover scales which are self-sufficient in certain respects and interdependent within certain operations as in nature.

We should define at least to closer approximation the scales of various operations for an individual, family and community in villages, towns and cities so that their mode of living is in relation to not only the diurnal cycle of 24 hours but also in relation to weekly, monthly, yearly needs. This way every individual who ultimately makes the community and the city has his own choice to work, rest, reflect and create.

It is necessary to repeat that we are building for Man. It is for Man that we should plan and urbanise, and it is for Man that we should design.

With today's technologies, it is easy to build a new world, which can link with the great past in terms of basic values and with the future in terms of convenience for the larger number.

Planning will only succeed, provided uncertainties about 'values' are reduced to a minimum and are not subject to pressure of circumstances. Fortunately, we are becoming aware of the consequences of our present day actions and we are dissatisfied and we do want to concern ourselves with after effects of industrialisation.

Our conflict is within our ideals so now we are beginning to realise that to face crisis against all odds, it is essential to preserve cultural heritage. And culture is made of values, material and spiritual.

To support this settlement, we have to recognise that technological advances and exploration of new avenues are necessary. It is of great importance to harness resources and energies to support the ever-increasing regional world population. We have not understood properly a place of technology. It is a tool, not the end in itself. But the tool has become a hammer which we can't wield. Unbridled technology has resulted in huge productions resulting in conspicuous consumption. Technology should be utilised in relation to Man's welfare.

It is time that we stop, pause and look for the wisdom we need, wherever we can find it.

Maybe, we should start thinking once again. And to this effect, I am putting a few thoughts before you for your deliberation.

First, I put before you some views of the late Professor L.P. Jacks.

Our main aim should be to become industrious not merely industrialised. By becoming industrious, ie through skill and healthy competition and choice to produce, we can have a better rapport between work that one enjoyed doing and leisure as its counterpoint. Our approach to both thus will be based on using life, time and space more fruitfully. With this goal our problems of quantity, ie solution for the largest numbers and immediately will be interlinked with quality. This will improve the values since quality will convert the quantity into an expression of life's desire and will not belong to the realm of competition because it will not be superfluous but is essential.

The purpose of industrialisation is to give man increasing leisure so that this quality of work through time and reflection will improve. He will, through appreciation of quality, enjoy his work and make his leisure not an idle pastime but a useful counterpoint. Work will no more become a curse but an aspiration. The people whose industry demonstrates the skill, the quality of its goods and makes possible the involvement of its people, is not merely industrial people. The lifestyle of such people due to qualitative thinking rises high and all work for them becomes art. Even quantity gradually tends to succumb to quality. Thus unwanted things disappear and every 'form' of environment becomes joy and an experience.

To this end, what sort of planning and architecture is most helpful to the so-called industrialising countries? What considerations should the professional have, so that its expressions have a bearing on the history and the culture of the people, with this in view of what planning we should have for a region? Should it be based on social expectations, religious faith, aesthetic outlook, or only on economic affluence? It is accepted that we as professionals, with limited field of control, cannot directly provide for the amelioration of economic condition. But it is possible that we may be able to so devise plans, that economic growth not only becomes possible but progressive. This we can do. On the other hand we may not be able to change the social customs and manners of a people, but we can plan so as to provide for a healthy observation of these. The architect-planner naturally cannot preach any religious doctrine, but whatever the religious form, he can plan and provide for the individual or for community either for prayers, for meditation for ceremonies or festivals.

As planners and architects our work should go beyond mere management of functions, spaces, technologies and form. The solutions need not be merely quantitative, but instead they should become qualitative. Quality demands time and a philosophy of values. However, it is necessary first to discover ways and means of achieving the immediate required quantity and then its gradual transformation in quality.

It is found that quite often there are areas around which people identify themselves and to them, this becomes the main theme. For example religion, community functions, cultural places become more significant than a mere shelter. Everything focuses around these. Quality in these areas is what one looks for. If such structures are discovered in our large- and small-scale planning it will be easier to establish an order around which all other activity such as housing, industry, education and culture can be built.

Quality in time will naturally emerge provided the entire process is generated with this faith. This is the basis of planning or architecture. This is what we call culture, and the structures around which people like to throng are the institutions of Man.

In short we should search for the main institutions which generate and give life its meaning. In planning and in architectural expression, this is what we have to work for.

I have put before you, as an Indian architect, my views and beliefs regarding planning and architecture. I know that here we are meeting at a place which is rightly proud of its hoary and magnificent culture. I believe we can learn much from it. In our discussions we should not forget that we are not in any upstart civilisation. This should make us modest.

LIMITS OF CITY GROWTH

1978

While I was reading the reports on the existing problems and growth needs of Cairo and Greater Cairo, I felt that I was reading documents on old and new Delhi, old and new Ahmedabad or old and new Hyderabad.

The reasons are simple.

Given the historical background of the above cities, their historical and cultural significance and their present state of development, one could perceive that the problems posed for Cairo and greater Cairo are almost identical, ie the unplanned expansion of cities are deteriorating the city fabric and hence these second thoughts on the new development. Since the problem is almost identical to some of our Indian cities which have a core – the old city – and its development around – the new city – I feel like raising a few questions.

1. Migration and its effects
Can the quality of a city with a cultural, economic and political past improve, if there is a constant influx of large population from the surrounding areas? It is known that through sheer desperation the migrants cause imbalances in the sociocultural texture of the city and build pressure and cause shortages in housing, infrastructural facilities and amenities.

2. Integrated development
Can existing planning strategies of further expanding of the cities as they are be reviewed in order to integrate development of the region as a whole? Will not the balanced and integrated development of the region reduce the disparity between the city and its surroundings and reduce migration to city?

3. Economic base
Can the city ever survive on its own resources when it has to procure its daily consumer and other items (vegetables, milk, raw materials etc) at economic cost from the surrounding region, particularly when the region is getting depleted of its population and resources, due to neglect and city expansion?

4. Old city and its culture
Can the integrated socio-economic culture existing within the old city be either uprooted or changed to reduce congestion through partial rehabilitation?

5. Human and other resources
Finally, should we not take into account the basic resources such as human beings, land and natural elements like water, air etc, to develop appropriate technology for more balanced development in various parts of the country and obtain better opportunities and environment for all? These questions, I am sure, are also raised in your country. Now I give my observations on the subject.

Sociocultural

A community lives by its culture. A city, being composed of many communities, offers choices of various cultural activities and attracts people from surroundings all over. However, culture is as much important as Man's economic survival. Hence the prerequisite of establishing community is to encourage social and cultural values. In fact all the historically known cities have preferred this cultural aspect along with economic, political or such other biases. There are several examples in our country which are not due to mere growth but due to over emphasis on economic and industrial growth. The tensions developed due to the new imbalance is being experienced by all our large and still growing cities such as Calcutta, Delhi, Bombay, Ahmedabad and Hyderabad.

It is also observed that no matter how much economic benefits are provided to Man, he is reluctant to leave his place of living, particularly the part of the old city. Since the sociocultural ties developed over generations, they have given him a sense of continuity and identity as well as a meaning to his life. It is also observed that 'security' is not necessarily monetary but it is the emotional security obtained through one's community. Even though the physical environment is substandard, happiness can be experienced through so many intangible ways.

Choice

This being the case, even the migrants from surrounding settlements prefer to survive in the old parts of the city rather than settle in new unidentifiable areas. It is found that it is more economical to survive in the old cities because of the nature and mode of local operations.

In the old city many operations are based on a small scale and are directly or indirectly related at several levels. Thus the fabric of such operations and transactions create many opportunities which can absorb additional or marginal employment. Though these operations are usually called 'unorganised' they in fact constitute almost 30% to 40% of the city's activities. The structure of such activities works on marginal amenities and on cultural ethos.

This fact, that the fabric of a city is woven at several levels of activity like a lattice and not as a conglomeration of operations seems to have remained unnoticed. Hence attempts to relieve the burden of the city through a transportation network or urban renewal or new expansions do not succeed but add a new dimension to the basic problem of the existing city. Two facts become apparent from this observation. First, the new development is usually much too loose, costly for people and does not take account of lifestyle and cultural patterns of the communities. Second, there is no emphatic attempt to rehabilitate the entire 'community' as a whole. We must recognise that people do not like to break totally from the traditional environs and move to socially unharmonious and insecure places.

The other consequences of this indiscreet expansion of the cities and the neglect of hinterland has shown us that the immigrant from the surrounding settlements with hardly any skills migrates to city for marginal work and thus aggravates and overburdens housing, infrastructure of the city and affects adversely the earlier city dweller. Strangely the addition of industry to the city, contrary to our belief, has deteriorated the existing standards of the city. If this is so, the obvious question is why do we allow our cities to expand?

The reason perhaps could be to centralise power or to have easy access to all facilities in order to achieve results in the shortest possible time; or should we say it is a lack of awareness or courage to develop surrounding areas and allow the cities to grow? Slow but overall pace of growth of the region usually does not find favour with the patrons? But one may ask if many people benefit today in the entire country by only expanding the cities?

Hence the question that we should ask is are our present strategies suitable to our country? Are there any other solutions or are there any models in our tradition which have survived for centuries that we can look to and get some inspiration for development. I would like to give you here two examples from my country. 1. A traditional settlement. 2. An old city.

From the examples it may be observed that the patterns of locations of settlements were and are even today very much related to the available communications, ie 6 to 7km walking distance. They are based on a viable economy as well as cultural interactions. For example, economic, religious and social activities occurring during a week, a month or a year were all related and structured on the basis of graded relationships between settlements, towns and cities. The settlements of diverse scales also specialised in their additional special functions such as commerce, industry, religion etc. In this system time, technology and economic development played a role appropriate to the total development of man, and his community. In short, there was a fundamental relationship of Man with the available 24 hours, his land and his tools which we call technology. There also was a firm belief of establishing hierarchy of institutions of Man in which public institutions were given priority to determine the scales of settlements.

In order to achieve this well-tried method of balanced development, systems of organisations were devised in which one could get choices to play the most effective role based on the capability and potentialities for development. One can see this reflected in the entire cultural activities such as planning, architecture, music, and activities of everyday life such as food, clothing etc.

This well-structured relationship of settlements and institutions has not only provided choices but also has an inbuilt sense of security and a well-developed value system. Even today villages, towns and cities if one looked in depth express this.

Since this well-knit integrated socio-economic structural pattern is still surviving and has a deeper meaning, I believe, that if we want to achieve a balanced and eventually faster economic growth, prevent deterioration and disparity in and between cities and settlements, it is essential to evolve a philosophy and a methodology for an integrated development. For example, we must look into potentials that are existing in each settlement including all urban centres and the surrounding areas. We must develop technologies which encourage the use of maximum local resources. For example, human beings are a large resource in our country and their capacity to learn skills is not being utilised fully. They reluctantly go to the city as unskilled labour but would prefer to be employed in industry which uses more efficient but appropriate technology. They would also prefer to have an input to short-circuit the daily operations which occupy their time. Today, new ideas developed in science and technology are possible to be transmitted to the remotest parts of the country through satellite communications and other systems.

With such regional development, several areas will have places which will provide facilities for work, education, business etc. These places will have enough attractions with better facilities to lead a wholesome life and a new network of growth centres will thus come into being.

Through such a development, migration to the overpopulated cities will not only be reduced but, if life is better nearby, the trend of migration from the city may eventually reverse. Many cities in the USA are showing this trend since the city very often does not offer better facilities to live with choice. Besides, mobility and communication systems are also available at other places, besides the metropolis.

To encourage this trend of limiting the growth of cities and encourage the development of the surrounding region it should be coupled with another strategy. To reallocate public institutions at different places, to decentralise cultural social and other activities based on frequencies to daily, weekly, monthly and yearly needs. To install these centres where particular important activities can take place.

Through this method cross-cultural contacts will be generated amongst the people and a fabric of activities similar to that of the old city will be obtained. I believe that this way of planning will provide several choices for the much demanded activities such as industrialisation and commerce and can be easily coupled with tourism and cultural exchange.

Therefore if we take the case of Cairo and Greater Cairo, I would like to venture and say that development of the surrounding region is more important than expanding only the existing city. There are of course many reasons for concentrating all new activities in Greater Cairo but as mentioned earlier, if we add additional activities, they will not only be an additional burden but will also not be able to solve the existing issues. It will, on the contrary, I think, further complicate the life of the Cairene citizen as well as the nation.

I also believe that beyond a certain size any addition which over-stresses the capacity will become a cause of direct and indirect economic burden to the surrounding region; and if simultaneous action for regional development is not undertaken the effects will be incurable. Hence it is necessary to tackle the problem from its root and take bold decisions which may appear slow to show results, but will have far reaching developmental and stabilising consequence on the nations as a whole.

ARCHITECTURE AND ATTITUDES

1979

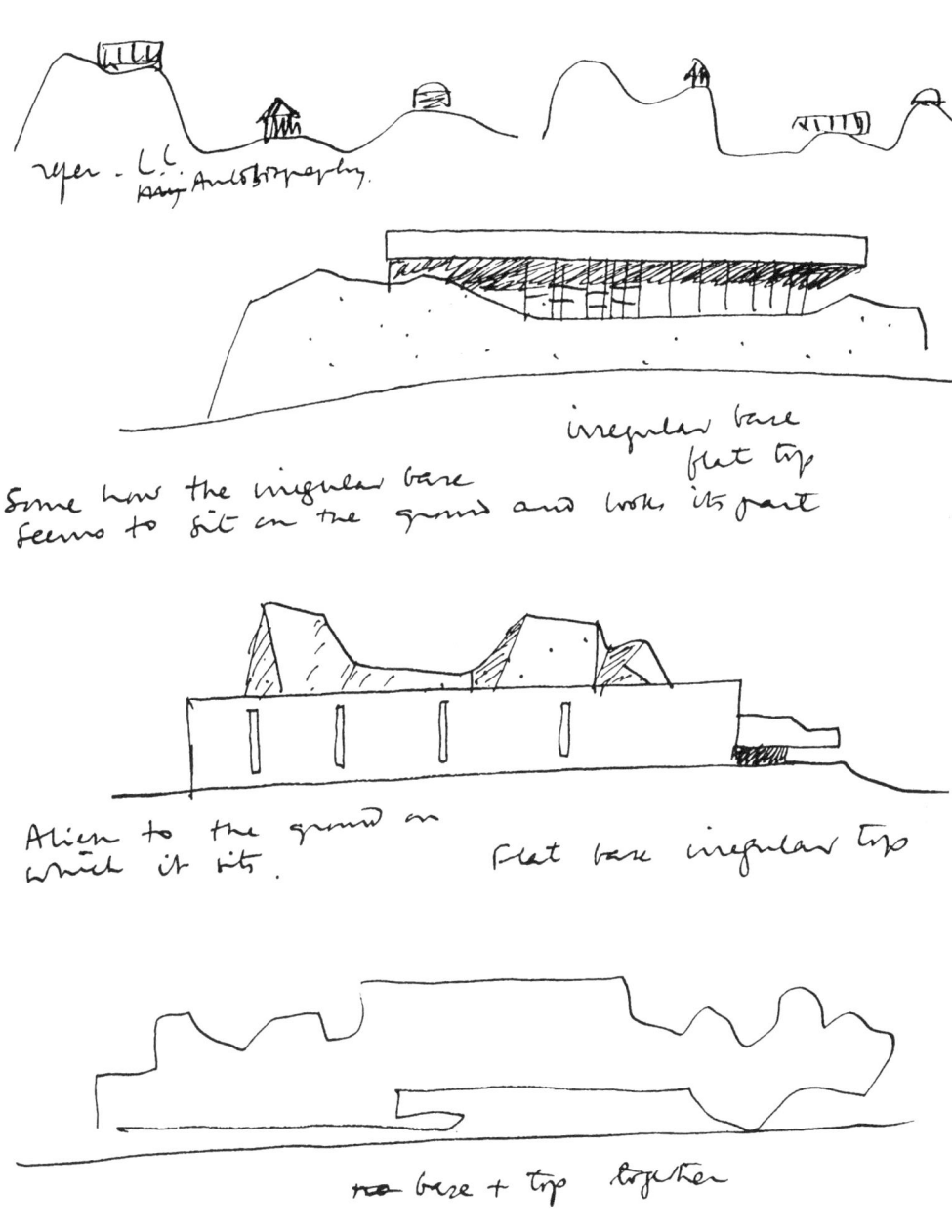

refer - L.C.
being Autobiography.

Some how the irregular base
seems to sit on the ground and looks its part

irregular base
flat top

Alien to the ground on
which it sits.

Flat base irregular top

base + top together

April 25/62

Anant.

It is a difficult task since architecture can be considered as a generalised art. We live inside and around it, see it and experience it. When it becomes familiar, we do not know what to say about it in terms of architecture, because with familiarity, we see and feel it as an extension of a lifestyle.

Architecture is also called the Mother of Arts. This, I presume, is because of its more permanent nature as compared to the other arts. Objects of daily use such as pottery, furniture, weaving etc, are relatively short-lived, even though they enrich our daily life. These articles can be changed whenever our fancy directs us. The products of other arts such as sculpture and painting generally existed as embellishments of buildings. On the other hand, once we build a house, it stays with us, perhaps with marginal modifications. We come across a great many houses which are generations old and still lived-in. In spite of their limitations, the heritage and the bond are strong enough to preserve and maintain them. It must, therefore, be recognised that the major differences between architecture and the other arts is the degree of encompassing symbolic value their products have for large groups of people over time.

Architecture survives through time, it remains longer and therefore it also helps us, through its expressions, to know about several aspects of lifestyles and hence of culture. The remains of Mohenjo-daro, Lothal, ancient places of Greece, even Ellora and Ajanta, through the house plans, the systems of drainage, water supply, tell us about the inhabitants and the culture they were part of.

Architecture survives through time because it demonstrates several phases of appropriateness rather than only a stylish expression based on personalities alone. It always offers a transition, and never a style which has taken deep root forever, but one which comes and passes away giving place to the new. Hence architecture has to be conceived after understanding life at several levels. It is like a village house which provides a shelter, but by itself is nothing except brick, asbestos roof or corrugated sheets, and therefore has all the possibilities of changes within and without, a continuous transition over several levels and phases.

In general, buildings take years to build. When they are finally completed some changes in values and attitudes may have taken place in the meantime, and we may have difficulty in adjusting to the earlier design. However, the building continues as a witness to our partial understanding of functions. It may not feel as good as we thought it would. On analysis we find that there are some elements which are relevant and should stay, some which should not.

I have been saying all these things just to focus on the permanence of architecture on the one hand and on the role it plays as a container of lifestyles and culture carried over through time, always allowing for continuous transitions on the other hand. Relationship with people makes it a generalised art and at the same time its ability to reflect the whole culture makes it the Mother of Arts. Hence it becomes very difficult to be sure about attitudes towards architecture. I have, however, come to some conclusions through my involvement in architecture over the last 25 years. I have learnt from Mons. Le Corbusier how to look at structure and functions. I have learnt from him how to create space out of these elements. He made me aware of technology and how to conceive a form in relation to the landscape around. Yet there are many other things that need to be learned, and it is never enough. Every time I have designed a building, I have realised that there are many things missing, and the buildings appeared alien, incomplete. They never appeared to have taken roots. This dissatisfaction at one's own creativity has raised many questions which I am always groping for answers to. I should perhaps try to elaborate on the things I have discovered and the things I have yet to find through the example of my works.

The illustrations of the two miniatures show the influence of climate on lifestyles. The Indian miniatures, local crafts and activities give us a clue of not only the climatic problems such as heat, sun, rain, or dust storms, but also tell us a great deal about ceremonies and festivals. They tell us about the ways the various elements of a building can be used, like porches, verandahs, open spaces, staircases, balconies, terraces etc. I realised the value of such lessons right from the beginning and have attempted to incorporate these in my designs.

To illustrate this in detail let me quote my efforts to design the Shreyas Campus. This was my first major project and was designed with the major idea of MAXIMUM FLEXIBILITY AND CONVERTABILITY OF SPACE WITH THE GREATEST ECONOMY. The classrooms were located separately and have no built-in covered corridors. The students walk through the open spaces and are able to observe trees, birds, the changing seasons, in other words, nature in its totality. Besides, unlike the typical classrooms, here I attempted to evolve a plan and an interior space which would be suitable for several activities for different age groups and would be economical also. In the structure of the classroom, a precast roofing technique with a special form was worked out, so that the interior space can have two different heights in the same space offering two different spaces for the children and the grown-ups. The roof was designed to create an air-space in between the two layers, one built of asbestos on top for water proofing, and the other of RCC. This keeps the interior spaces cool, provides for easy cross-ventilation and good light. In addition to this technique providing comfort from the climate, the centrally pivoted windows for the classrooms were built to diffuse or direct the light. The overhands in the roof protect the building from sun and rain. As economy plays a great role in India, it was essential to build at minimum cost.

Another element I learnt to value a great deal is the SURROUNDING LANDSCAPE. For example, when I designed my house in 1960, I felt that my house should be a demonstration in developing compatible landscapes. I wanted to show ways to my neighbours whose houses were also to be built at the same time as mine and with the same requirements. Indirect light, protection to the walls, insulation through the use of cavity walls, were some of the innovations I used to get around the climatic problems. I found also that trees all around the house insulate the house immensely. The difference in the temperature within the house and outside is in the range of 8 to 12 degrees F in the summer. Landscaping, particularly the presence of trees, is a must to help in creating and improving the environment, and more comfortable living conditions.

In my house one can see how a diffused light within and avoidance of direct sunlight have been made possible by improving upon the traditional *chhaja* which normally projects only horizontally from walls. I modified the chhaja and created a light-catcher to bring indirect light within the house. During summer afternoons one can remain inside the room in comfort by closing all the doors. Usual glass windows have been avoided. The diffused light expresses the volume better, giving the interior special tonality rather than the sharp-edged light.

I also decided to have a variety of space inside as well as a feeling of extended space from inside the house to the outside. When the doors are opened, the house becomes a pavilion and both the inside and outside spaces become continuous. The staircases which are normally isolated from the main living space is made a part of the house in order to become multi-functional and more useful during larger gatherings.

While designing the Institute of Indology, I was faced with the task of insulating the manuscripts from varying temperatures. I discovered that the best and most economical way to do this was to have a basement for the manuscripts, where the temperature variations are at a minimum. The other intention in the design of the building was to CREATE A FORM THAT WOULD EVOKE A FEELING OF TRADITION. A verandah all around the large gathering hall on the first floor was built to create a traditional form, the feeling of familiarity, and additional space for movement. The building was constructed in concrete frame for economy. To accomplish this, large structural spans were used to provide flexible space for varied activities. The H-shaped columns carry services. In this building, I tried to create an expression of form, structure and technology representing the local ethos in totality.

Concepts of GROWTH AND CHANGE are other very important aspects of design and architecture, particularly in India. Due to the fluctuating economic situations, building projects in India are often uncertain affairs. Be it a house, a university,

an office building or a factory, projects usually start off with grand plans, but by the time construction begins either the prices have gone up or the required funds could not be raised or perhaps some unforeseen situation has cropped up to limit the scope of the original plans. I have come across many such cases and have tried to evolve some solutions for them. In the design of laboratories for the Gujarat University a pattern for its future growth and expansion is taken into account in the basic concept. Then the services and structure were integrated to make each unit as a model. The basic design provides great flexibilities for the expansion of the building both vertically and horizontally. This design not only saves energy and costs, but also creates a feeling of completeness at every phase of growth.

I believe that a building should never appear neglected or incomplete. Since this occurs frequently in India, every architect must make it a basic principle to be aware of this problem. In fact in all developing countries this problem is common. Even in the Middle Eastern countries where there is no shortage of money this problem occurs. There, architects and designers talk of schemes having phases of growth and a capacity to expand.

I will quote another example where I have attempted to overcome this problem. While designing the GSFC office building I provided for a basic unit which can grow vertically floor by floor in contrast to the traditional rectangular office building where to increase even one department, it becomes necessary to add an entire floor which often creates difficulties in adjustments with existing departments. In the GSFC office building, each department is housed in one block, and the department can grow vertically keeping the linkages with other departments housed in similar separate blocks.

Living in India and being acquainted with villages and the villager's customs and cultures, I have realised that things which are normally not considered part of design are also equally important. Considerations to accommodate VARIABLE FUNCTIONS FOR A SPACE OR SPACES for different economic and social groups are essentials in the design process. The greater the area of considerations, the more harmonious is the result. An isolated view of nonfunctional design, on the other hand, can destroy the overall efficiency of an organisation or a system. I feel tempted to quote here Mr Charles Eames, appreciation of the *lota* with its design as an expression of many nuances of use and feelings. It is blended to the Indian way of life because it is designed to fulfil various needs of day-to-day living.

In the process of creating built environments there are not only measurable and conceivable elements that affect the building in the long run, but also many immeasurable and inconceivable elements. In architecture one must view the ENVIRONMENT AS A TOTALITY OF BUILDINGS AND NATURAL SPACES TOGETHER. The tradition and culture become most important forces to bring them together and enable the buildings to take root, to survive.

Indian culture, through its several socio-economic ramifications, gives a sense of security, while allowing wide choices. In the traditional Indian society, one is not alone, but part of a community. Hence, buildings are not built in isolation, but in groups leading to a total environment. A merger of buildings, spaces and culture. The community shares everything, whether economic activities or the social festivals. Unless the sociocultural tradition is understood, the location of buildings, streets, spaces and their forms cannot be accommodated into the desired fabric wherein the community wants to live.

It is, therefore, necessary to talk about PHYSICAL ENVIRONMENT IN TERMS OF CULTURE rather than only in terms of buildings, space, technology or economy. For example, the house form which has evolved in India, say in Ahmedabad, has behind it centuries of tradition. This tradition not only ties the community of one generation together, but also the generations within the house. In the house plans, it is difficult to perceive this immediately, but seen though the minute activities and functions carried out in the house, it can be realised, rather felt, that a sense of identity are all there. These must be preserved in designing new environments and to do this it is necessary to understand the sociocultural patterns.

The illustration of a simple village well as an element representing a sociocultural pattern has often been quoted. The well is an institution which binds the community very strongly because this is where people meet each other daily, discuss their problems, find solace in their griefs, and feel socially cared for. There are a large number of such manifestations in the old and existing institutions which tell us about the sociocultural tradition of the community. Detailed study of these can provide us with a genuine understanding of the real needs to be given importance by architecture and design.

To me, therefore, INSTITUTIONS ARE THE PRIMARY DESIGN ELEMENTS in creating an environment. I have come to the conclusion that religious institutions, particularly the temple, through ages have influenced greatly the community environment. There are temple cities in the South, as well as in the North, which have survived for centuries because the religious institutions have provided the community with cultural stability, security, occupation and guidance in its behavioural patterns. These also helped in establishing value systems and a strong conviction in continuous community belonging. This was a great lesson to me, and as I continued to learn this, I have tried to stress on public institutions and community activities while planning and designing housing or townships.

I have also learnt that only having institutions are not enough. For the institutions to survive, grow, expand and be a part of the culture, there must be an ORGANISATIONAL STRUCTURE EVOLVED BY THE SOCIETY. I have discovered that in the Ajanta and Ellora caves, while the building activity continued over centuries, the quality of execution and the craftsmanship continued to get better. Today, the work assigned to an assistant or to a contractor cannot achieve the expected quality if the designer is absent for even a few months. But in the case of these caves and temples, the chief architect or the *sthapati* used to come, stay for a year and then go away. He perhaps would not come again, but the work went on through generations, with the quality remaining constant and often improving.

Year	Type of Work	Concept and its basic motive	realisat	Degree of Success

Siting

Form on Site.

volumes

Surface textures

Rhythm

internal volumes

materials in terms of

colour + texture + scale

Structural Technic form + function

Oct 14/61

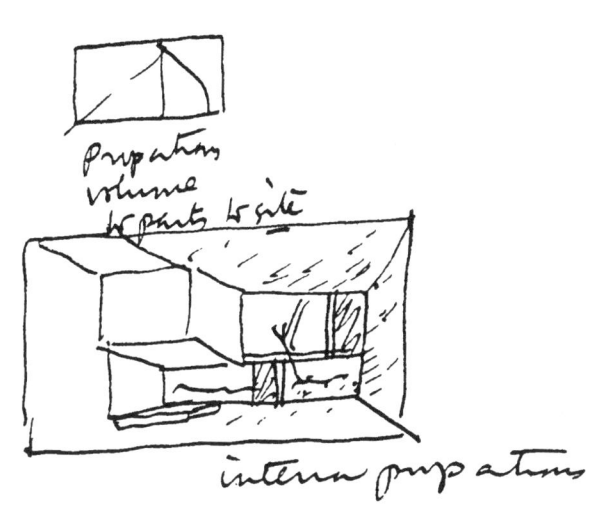

proportions
volume
of parts to site

internal proportions

*— Architecture is always effective
if the use of light   must TIE together
   use of volume
   use of spatial relationships
is just right
Surface textures - etc can be
then tackled with descretion
           NOV 19/61

This process had within it the built-in mechanism of COMMUNITY COMMITMENT AND CONVICTIONS passed down through generations. The generations of designers, builders and craftsmen would continue to build the institution, each excelling the previous one, motivated by their commitment to remain true to the major principles, and guidelines, established by the *sthapati* with regard to the location, the materials, the technology, the design of the carvings, the sense of depth. This example suggests that within a main concept, an organisational system and a method must be developed to continue the work, to provide choices for participants to identify themselves with the work and thus generate excellence. This quality of transition, of commitment to the community, and ability and sanction to interpret principles by individuals are very much in contrast to the contemporary Western philosophy. There, perhaps, greater importance is given to the individual and his role, and not to the organisation. People there, I presume, believe that when the individual dies, the end of the organisation also comes.

It is interesting to see therefore why Indian culture has survived through many centuries and why it is good in some ways. This is because through centuries institutions have evolved along with the living environment and have provided a broad FLEXIBLE STRUCTURE in which an individual has the 'choice' to interpret in his own way. As a result, the commitment to the concept of community has been deep-rooted and this has tended to provide for total harmony. The built-in variations in all aspects of Indian life and activity creation provide always an open and, with regard to growth, evolution and change. This is another very important aspect I wish to emphasise. In our modern attitude to development planning, building and designing, these issues are basic and often ignored when preconceived or imported strategies are attempted to be followed. These strategies do not work and hence become totally inefficient.

Such attitudes to organisation, structure and design can be discovered in Indian architecture, particularly that of the temples which have served as the most important CATALYTIC INSTITUTION TO PRESERVE THE CULTURE. In Indian architecture, the creators, the designers, thought many functions other than just simply the basic functions should be performed by the building. For example, the idea of a staircase performing only the function of movement, a window that of lighting and ventilation, or a roof that of providing shelter from the weather, are basically alien to Indian culture since such cannot satisfy the diverse needs of diverse groups. A staircase can mean many things – a place to sit, if bigger perhaps a place to sleep.

ALL ELEMENTS MUST BE CONSIDERED THEREFORE AS MULTIFUNCTIONAL. That is what Indian culture has grown with and that is how the Indian temperament is built. GROWTH OR BUILDING ARE NOT JUST ADDITIVE, BUT ARE BASIC TO THE BALANCED LIFE. Therefore all elements of the environment must be designed to satisfy more than one situation.

Architecture and design of today must incorporate this concept which is so strongly rooted in our culture. All elements must be considered as alive, as dignified, as flexible. That is how all objects of art in India through ages have given birth to a typical environment and sustained the culture and in the process has sustained itself.

As I have stated earlier, with each passing year I am becoming more perceptive and am trying to achieve the things I have just talked about. I shall now attempt to illustrate some of these efforts of mine.

In the Bhadra area of Ahmedabad we designed the Premabhai Hall. This is the area where the city of Ahmedabad started growing first. Located on the bank of the river, this area included the Azam Khan Palace and the Bhadrakali Temple. Opposite this place was the central open area and on the axis leading to the east are the three gates, beyond which are located the Jumma Masjid and the King's and Queen's tombs. In between the palace and the gates was the Great Maidan. This *maidan* was gradually encroached upon by shopping activities and bazaar and in due course housing were also added. In our proposal we are aspiring to bring the old grandeur of this maidan which in the early days inspired most of the community activities, recreations and pastimes. We are also aspiring to revive the original grandeur around the palace. For this it was necessary that we study the traffic pattern, the occupations of the inhabitants of the area and their activities. We have since proposed a new scheme with due considerations to the present activities and the revival of the past functions of this area. In our plan we have proposed relocation of these activities at different places within the same area giving the municipality or the developing authority more area for use and revenue and also to provide the city with a breathing space it so badly needed. Our proposal of shopping areas, new office premises and re-routing the traffic will not only bring additional revenue, but will, we believe, improve the quality of life in this area.

As architects, our task is not only difficult but time consuming. This project (the Premabhai Hall) has been with us since 1958, and it was completed only in 1975–76. During these 18 years I not only changed the concept seven or eight times, but I had also to solve the problem of land acquisition as well as the problem of locating the building on the site. Besides, I had to persuade the clients to take into account the development of the surrounding areas. All these take a long time.

The total renewal scheme for this area that we have now proposed may take 15 to 20 years. And in the process of developing the final designs I came across many technical and non-technical problems. We have phased the scheme in parts with a hope to build the hall and initially a plaza and create a place for the city, which eventually will become larger. The decisions in the first phase were very crucial, because we had to deal with monuments all around and develop our plan in relation to the temple and the fort wall.

The question was can we really build something new alongside these monuments, and if so, what should be the nature of our design so as to preserve the character of the old on the one hand and yet express the technology of today through the new building and the plaza around? The problem was to integrate these two conditions. The great task was to bring the present and the past together in a living relationship.

In our scheme of the Hall we have attempted to answer some of these crucial issues. The top floor of Premabhai Hall is quite high and has a 20-foot-long cantilever. I was attempting to relate the walls of the hall to the *Bhadra* area and to the profile of the fort wall, with the belief that the fort should be seen. Besides, the new building should not overpower the palace and the fort.

Other considerations while designing the project were the functions, which were many. However, we had to explore how the quality of the building could be changed to look light and articulated enough without becoming stylish. Here the designer has to discover once again the virtues of blank planes. To achieve this effect, articulation of spaces and the planes is needed. Particularly in the case of the left facade on the street which was treated to express a lesser mass. If openings were made on the side, if balconies were added, the wall would have changed its scale and looked big for the setting. Hence it is left blank and made less significant and easy to look at. The overall form of the building with its end walls is designed to look almost like an animal standing still. The profile of the wall with the openings therein are made to articulate the surface. Concrete has been used as the principal structural material for the entire building.

An architect works with functions and while handling them takes into account the inner relationships which exist between them, besides taking care of things like insulation, lighting etc, in this building the staircases are located on the periphery and the auditorium at the centre. The staircases not only insulate the interior from heat, thus reducing the cost of the air conditioning, but also continues the movement of space with relation to the outside world. As an architect, one is constantly trying to manipulate functional elements which are constant and tries to give a characteristic expression to the building. For example, the staircase located on the periphery is reflected on the outside wall and has given the building a form totally different and useful.

Fortunately, in India we have plenty of natural light and even though artificial light is necessary in theatre interiors we have tried to use natural light as and when possible. We have tried to bring natural light into public areas by separating the main auditorium from the peripheral structure.

The central space is very important in public halls, because it can be used by everybody, like the ones in the temples. I believe that the central spaces should belong to those who come to the plaza as well as those who come to the theatre. These spaces could be fruitfully used for exhibitions, lectures, seminars etc, like those which used to go on in the temples. Even the staircases located on both the sides of the central foyer of the hall merge with it and thus make it accessible to all visitors.

A second project I wish to mention is the Central Bank of India building in Ahmedabad. The clients wanted to put up a traditional bank building but the central location of the site demanded many considerations, important amongst which were its relationship to the surrounding gardens, streets and historical monuments. Future traffic patterns of the growing city also had to be considered. Hence, we proposed to create a pedestrian walk at a height of 20 feet where we located a restaurant, a little auditorium and possible linkages to other buildings. These linkages located 20 feet above ground could connect the spaces around the Lal Darwaja. This way the whole area, including the Parekhs and right up to Bhadra could be linked so that pedestrians could move at that level, go down to the bank or to the commercial areas, and up to the upper levels for the offices or houses. With this concept in mind, the form of the building was evolved. Consequently, the large flight of stairs from the street to the plaza, going up 20 feet, links the two main functions of the bank building and also suggests future pedestrian linkages. This large staircase becomes a connection between the activities in the building and those on the street and removes the isolation of the building and integrates the inside with the outside. The outside activities thus become part of the building.

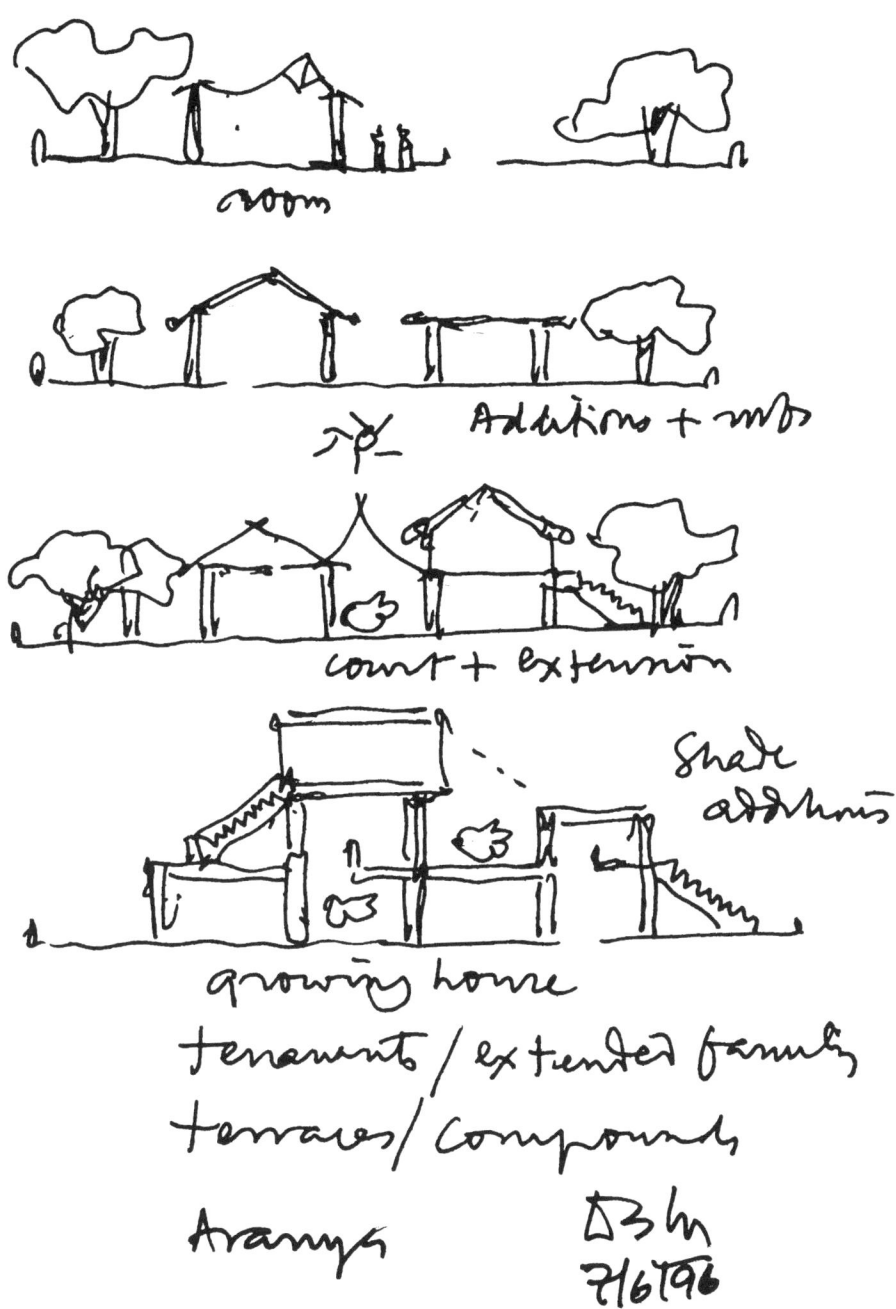

Designing houses and public buildings is the common activity of an architect. I have gradually come to realise, however, that such designs are not very interesting unless they also have larger significance. So gradually I have shifted to the design of larger complexes like industrial townships or housing projects. This way, I am attempting to find for myself some answers to the many questions relating to the larger groups and having wider planning implications rather than only the architectural issues. I am convinced that in this process one can fulfil an important aspect of design which is the integration of choices of participants besides clients and designers. Also a large number of others such as graphic artists, potters and local craftsmen can participate to add variety to the total endeavour.

In 1964, I was commissioned to design the township for the Gujarat State Fertilizer Co, Ltd (GSFC) near Baroda. In such townships, the design problems are very complex. For example, take the question of design of the houses. Aside from the actual design of the individual buildings, we had to consider the fact that the future occupants would be coming from as many as seven different income groups. Rents were to be subsidised and the designs had to reflect the future occupants differing abilities to afford the space. Unfortunately, the requirement for shelter is not related to the family needs of income. It is known that the lower the income, the bigger is the family, but as a rule the house is smaller, related to what they can afford. This is a built-in paradox.

The second important condition is the differing patterns of living of the different communities who come to work from all over the country in such massive, industrial complexes. The variations in the patterns of living compels one to design for segregated conditions to avoid emotional conflicts. Therefore, the two factors of income variation and living pattern variation work together to avoid a mixed grouping. Consequently, the house type that has been allotted defines the status of the inhabitants and vice versa. Though undesirable, this is the general trend in most such townships. Hence while planning one should go into all the relevant social issues to clarify one's own perspective and to attempt to minimise the levels of conflicts.

In 1958 while designing houses for ATIRA I had discussed these issues with Dr Kamala Choudhry and the late Dr Sarabhai. They were one with me in recognising that single group housing has social ramifications and hence these need to be resolved through proper planning. In 1964, in the GSFC housing, I wanted to find ways by which there will be a lot more interactions between various groups through organising functions and physical elements. Though each of the seven types were located in separate clusters, my effort was to club them together wherever the lifestyles were found to be similar. Two major clusterings were created, one comprising house types 2 and 3 with standard bays so that they look almost similar. The site plan with all the houses was designed in such a way that the spaces between the clusters could be used by the children as play areas and for social and religious festivals and ceremonies. In this way it was hoped that segregation of caste, creed and status could be minimised. By the creation of central public spaces, I further sought to duplicate the spirit that such spaces have in the villages, where everyone can get an opportunity to meet and to interact. To achieve this I grouped all the non-residential facilities, like the shopping areas, the water tower, a cultural place, the schools, together. I was not sure whether such a system would work, but happily I find now that the concept of central cultural space, and spaces, and spaces between clusters, have been very successful. As a matter of fact, they have now even acquired a symbolic value.

Over the past few years, I have found also that people prefer to invest money in public areas, where they go on adding new buildings, new activities and more facilities. The company also does not mind investing money either for the same purpose. As in the illustration one can notice that the shopping has grown in years. The gardens around the tank is improving and recently added the new public auditorium.

It may be worthwhile to mention that the water tower initially was to hold only water and have no other function. But I argued that a staircase up to 100 feet would be very exciting and people could go up, relax and view the surrounding landscapes as well as the township. This area of the water tank, with a platform

and steps leading to it, has become a place for festivals. Today, the water tank has become a real central place like a temple of old, surrounded by a shopping area, an auditorium, a restaurant and a school of houses. The central complex with its tank can be seen from miles around, and within the township it serves as a landmark and a place to rendezvous. Incidentally, the cost of the water tank with the added elements came to only 20% more than it would have been as originally specified. So, if the levels of interaction observed today are any indication, the large open spaces and the public activity areas provided for in the plan compensated significantly for the lack of the same in the small house.

While the construction of houses was going on, the landscape was set, with specific emphasis on tree planting. Today there are close to 80 thousand trees in the township. Shade once imagined has today become a reality. The narrow streets between the houses have also become shaded areas for children to play in besides giving shaded access to the homes and open spaces. The streets and the open spaces thus have become important community spaces also.

For the larger more expensive executive houses we have a different type of clustering. Four to eight houses are planned around a common courtyard where the families meet. These houses have their own large gardens. However, as stated earlier, elements like verandahs, terraces and open spaces are common to all, only the scale is varied.

While I have highlighted on the success of the plan just discussed, I have since discovered that there are still many things missing, for example compound walls, adequate density of dwelling and inhabitants for proper interactions, vocational centres, etc. I have attempted to incorporate these elements in the housing I designed for the Electronics Corporation of India Ltd (ECIL) at Hyderabad, which I will now illustrate.

In the ECIL Housing at Hyderabad, I proposed that not only should there be public institutions, but also such institutions which can provide activities and employment for the relatives of ECIL employees. A vocational centre was therefore added to the layout of the township. To make this centre a focus of the township, the general layout was made as an open-ended spine with the centre located at the end. The main bus stop was also located there. The vocational centre and other activities located here can become places to learn, earn and interact with the outside world. This provides also significant impetus to all dwellers, and many outsiders as well, to do more.

While designing the housing, I had the opportunity to discuss the problems of income segregated housing with the late Dr Sarabhai, then the Chairman of the Department of Atomic Energy. With his concurrence it was possible to avoid separate clusters for different types of houses. In the ECIL, the housing is not only mixed, but each house has a lot more advantages than the ones designed for the GSFC. Houses here have better courtyards, easy access to the community spaces and hence more interaction.

As always, people are happier with public spaces than with their houses, since these areas have higher levels of utility and are much larger also. In the ECIL housing we provided for primary and secondary schools on the highest elevation, shopping in the central area and an amphitheatre, the club and a multipurpose hall in between. There is a small restaurant in the shopping area. One has to go through the shopping area and the school to the multipurpose hall. There is also a larger health centre, a post office, a bank and a fire station. All these buildings have become very important to the people. Similar to the GSFC pattern, the central space in the ECIL township has also become the heart of the township for the community interaction, activities and recreations.

The design of the houses was conceived to cause them to merge with the surroundings. Due consideration was given to the local climate, customs and building types and materials, and their relation to local traditions were given preference. The outcome was that the new buildings in the township came up with low profiles and the cost also fell within the very minimum as stipulated by the government. It need not be emphasised how important a constraint these stipulations can be. But constraints are seldom really limitations, in fact they can be seen as virtues which lead to success. The designer, through the scope of the challenge, can become more creative.

In the ECIL housing no special effort was needed to create a landscape. The sheet rock outcropping provided us with a natural landscape within which and without disturbing it, the buildings have been accommodated. The different levels of the land were wholly retained and were linked by means of steps. Thus the shopping area, the school, the public building, the amphitheatre and the housing could be placed within the natural topography, enhancing the aesthetic experience.

Both in the GSFC township and the ECIL township, I have observed that people are very happy with the public areas which we created. People visiting these places come back and tell me that the central spaces and the public spaces are the ones they like most. The institutions within the public spaces are the permanent elements, elements which through history have proved themselves to be the most important catalytic agents of human and community interactions. The architect, to be a good designer for the community living, must give the required priority and emphasis to building institutions which mould, steer and lift the community life.

While designing a mixed housing for the ECIL township, I discovered that apart from the usual questions of orientation, plans etc, each building type should be developed with its own characteristic function and in relation to the outdoor space. I have learnt through experience that the outdoor spaces provide much greater potential for evolving than the space within the house. The indoor spaces can vary from person to person over a period of time, but are of a more permanent nature, while the outdoor space, irrespective of income, caste, creed and community, can be modulated with greater convenience. I was convinced therefore that the outdoor space must be designed with greater consideration.

I have also given due consideration to the problem of expansion of the house. While designing the houses, I felt that the house must have either a central court or a court at one end, to allow for the extension of the house. The court can also become more useful as a result. The house is designed with the kitchen and the bath as the basic units.

In the space around this unit, walls can be built, a roof added, and a room is the result. This way the house can grow. This concept, though perhaps unconventional, is valid and if the technique is economical, if construction is easy to follow, then perhaps the idea will spread. Traditional housing structures in India are based on this very concept.

We tried to use precast techniques for the roofs so as to build the houses faster and at cheaper cost. The walls we built with local stone. The plan illustrated here indicated the load-bearing walls of the staircase, living room, bedroom, kitchen and bath and shows a curtain wall between bedroom and living room which can be removed if desired. The service area which forms the core of the house creates courts in the front and the rear which are linked with adjoining houses in order to obtain a garden for each home. In my studies I have seen that the old houses in Hyderabad and in the Maula Ali area where the ECIL township is located are small, but with courtyards, hence I followed the same concept. The staircase in each house becomes important and makes a compound wall and / or partition between the courtyards of two houses. The staircases have become an element of composition, and element of definition of space. Using the staircase, and providing to even the smallest house of 400 square feet area, two rooms and terraces open to the sky, I have attempted to recreate the clusters we find in traditional housing.

However, even in this ECIL housing, I find after completion that many issues have not been very clearly resolved. The outside skin of the wall has become heavy. The precast roof is not expressed outside and hence the roof does not cast shadows on the walls. And we have not provided balconies which have a characteristic of their own.

In conclusion I would like to say that with increasing experience and the perspective it brings me, I am becoming more and more convinced that no community and no society has a total list of its needs and requirements which can be a guideline for a designer of community living, of environment, to follow rigidly. But, at the same time, there are innumerable basic requirements for people of different caste, creed and status which the concerned groups demand as part of their living environment and it is the duty of the designer to find expressions for these. An architect and a designer interprets these demands as desires for expression of attitudes, and the architect and designer considers his mission a success, if in his design he can incorporate these demands. Does he, however, realise that in this process he is moving away from the philosophy of a designer, which is not only to design and to build, but also to work for the creation of a total environment where caste, creed and status are not the focal point but that the environment must be for everybody?

I am therefore convinced that an architect and a designer has a much larger role to play in the community, the society, than what he does today. He should not just be a vehicle for the expression of different attitudes, but must be, through his skill and ingenuity, a builder of attitudes also. He must be the agent to inculcate amongst all an attitude to live with others, rather than simply consolidating only the attitude to live. His design must have a place for everybody, and must offer everyone a role to participate in the building process of the total environment. That is why I believe that an architect and a designer must use the highest tools to 'create an attitude' for a total living environment. History has taught us this lesson, and the growing disintegration of today is the result of breaking away from institutions. We must revive these institutions, we must bring them back to the forefront, and we must in due course, put them back at the focal point of design if we want the society and the community to continue its advancement, where everybody is given his share of the living environment, and with this share the attitude for which living together can be born.

TOWARD AN APPROPRIATE LIVING ENVIRONMENT: QUESTIONS ON ISLAMIC DEVELOPMENT

1980

During the last three days we witnessed presentations on educational, institutional and recreational buildings by the architects. Dr Ul Haq has spoken of economic and Mr Soedjatmoko of social issues, and there were also many other speakers. The main thrust of the discussion following each presentation related to how each architect had understood Islamic traditions, and how he integrated these into his designs. Other questions were related to the way a project became part of the urban fabric and the community. The answers to these questions were not really convincing, at least not to the non- architects, because the solutions did not specifically indicate the relationship of a project to the social life of an area.

Dr ul Haq made very pertinent comments on the crucial issues of the Islamic Third World and the poverty of the masses. He asked if the architects were involved in solving the problem of shelter for that 80% of the population, or were giving them some alternatives of hope. Dr ul Haq's remarks, preceded by questions from other experts, opened many avenues of discussion extending beyond the topic of the present seminar. However, from these discussions a few questions come to my mind:
1) What is the Islamic tradition?
2) What are the lessons which we can extract from it?
3) Should the development imperative only be beneficial to a few, or should society at large be the focus?
4) Should there be a dependence on borrowed technology, or should there be an emphasis on local wealth, resources and skill?
5) Should there be a concern for the immediate future, or should the long-term perspective be given equal importance?

I will try to answer these questions one by one. It is important to recognise that Islamic culture originated and consolidated under the most severe environmental conditions in the world. Lack of resources and a scarcity of almost everything motivated Islam to establish a few very fundamental principles of life, such as dignity of labour, humility and dedication to God through work. This further evolved into a sense of participation, which through cooperation and equality became pronounced. Interdependence became one of the main principles. Scarcity also taught restraint and contentedness, with a feeling of gratitude to the unknown Almighty who provides mankind with the essentials and the inner strength to be happy with them. Devotion and dedication became the primary considerations for the well-being of the community instead of the individual, and tensions of inequality were avoided.

Basic cultural values found their expressions both in terms of behaviour of the individual and the community, and of the forms and structures which shelter them. The expressions that can be very clearly identified in the Islamic behavioural codes are: simplicity (ways of living and aspirations); adaptability (with limitations and constraints); participation (to generate the most from scarce resources); cooperation (united efforts to survive); humility (contentedness with life); devotion (gratefulness to the unknown who provides for us all); stability (through minimum aspirations) and security (through a sense of tolerance, brotherhood and self-reliance).

Simplicity, adaptability, participation, continuity, equality and a sense of stability became the canons of architecture. These canons were interpreted in terms of building design and forms, and gave rise to the unique architectural expression which we know as Islamic architecture. Because their attributes were so direct and meaningful even when built in another culture, the quality of Islamic architecture remained similar; it even adopted the local pattern or style for its expression without losing the principal message. The attempt to establish the concept of non-directional design modules to allow for intermingling of major and minor spaces, provide for easy communication and facilitate the religious, educational or cultural activity of the community, emphasised the fact that constraints are virtues and need not be abandoned.

The innumerable varieties of mosques, *madrasas, khāns* and *caravanserais* discussed in the last few days demonstrate the adaptability of changing needs. Not only that, but the basic principles mentioned above have been fitted to a variety

Udaipur
Jan 10/63

May 63

of sites and integrated with the surroundings. The modular structural system had the capacity to emphasise hierarchy with subtle nuances, and the total unity of this formal and often amorphous complex expressed the presence of the Supreme through the articulation of space, form and light. The quality of simplicity for individual use on the one hand, and magnificence of public buildings for the community on the other, provided a dual sense of equality in the community and gave unrestricted accessibility to all. In short, it was the outward expression of maximum benefits with minimum input; it achieved more with less, and anonymity while imparting divinity and grace. These principles saw the evolution of different architectural styles and different countries, and contributed to each culture in a particular way. This contribution, this ability to enrich the other culture, is what makes Islamic architecture great. We can summarise the Islamic tradition by saying that constraint is a virtue and that we can successfully achieve the design of desired goals if they are related to the community at large.

The second question asks what lessons can be drawn from the Islamic tradition for our present work. Islamic architecture's answer to this is simplicity and anonymity; that is, solutions designed with humility can absorb the prevalent cultural ethos as well as impart the qualitative aspect to the viewer. The idea of simplicity in design for the common dwelling is another message conveyed, as opposed to the provision of grandeur in the mosque or public institutions. The message therefore is that institutions are most important, and deserve the highest priority and all the energy and wealth we put into them to glorify hope and salvation.

My third question asks if the development imperative should be beneficial to only a few, or if society at large should be the focus. The answer lies in the Islamic conduct of commitment to equality; it should be asserted to re-establish social cohesion and stability. Muslim society as a whole should be the focus, and this will require that society prepare itself for the benefits of development. This will perhaps take time, and development will therefore have to be based on priorities with a different base; in short, priorities and scales should be established.

The fourth question was whether dependence on borrowed technology should be complete, or whether emphasis should be placed on local wealth, resources and skills. The answer follows clearly from the above. If benefits can accrue only when the adaptation of new technology is made possible, it follows that adaptation will grow out of both participation and a local wealth of resources and skills. Society at large suggests minimum dependence on borrowed technology; this in turn suggests that building design solutions not be very high-technology oriented, unless they are capable of being assimilated into the culture and also, preferably, employ local skills.

The final question I wish to address is: Should there be concern for the immediate future, or should the long-term perspective be given equal importance? There is only one answer, to my way of thinking. Benefit for society at large is paramount, and therefore a slow pace of development and a long-term perspective are required. Short-term goals compel a society to maximise gains, but they destroy local resources and skills in the process. This also leads to a decline in self-reliance and the loss of economic, and consequently, social independence. Preservation and conservation therefore become very vital. In short, our designs should be based on local potentials, with reliance on external help being minimised to encourage public participation rather than exclusive monopoly controls.

Let us recapitulate the issues. Constraint is a virtue and it must be the basis of design. Institutions are the backbone of society, and they must have the highest priorities in the development process. Buildings should avoid sophisticated technologies if not capable of assimilation, and reduce importation of materials in order to remain self-sufficient. Unfortunately, in contrast to these ideas, we are faced today with contradictions to the development process. They include rapid economic growth and an urge to create an environment comparable to that of the West; the fear that if material well-being and impressive development are not achieved, even the freedom of the society and the culture will be under strain; and finally, a mad rush for rapid change, with an ambition to achieve in a decade what the West could not achieve in a century. These are heightened by the fact that the control of decision making rests in the hands of a few, and the newly formed wealth is not shared by many.

This is the dilemma, and the only way to go about realising the ideals of Islamic culture is to make the clients or the decision makers aware. They need to be convinced of the long-lasting qualities of the Islamic heritage so they can direct development strategies accordingly. There are many alternatives that we can explore and follow, but the one that comes to my mind in the context of the present seminar is the following: attempts must be made to convince the decision makers that if they wish to achieve the Islamic order, they must take into account not only today's problems, but also their eventual spiraling in times to come. They must be made aware of the existence of the backbone of Islam, that is, the institutions and their priority in the process of development. 'Institutions' does not denote a mere building with a particular function, but signifies in a wider sense the place of such an edifice in the daily life and movement of a community. It is through these institutions that people generate a cultural ethos apart from mere economic development.

The workshop conclusions highlighted these issues and explained the role that they can play. If this institutional role is understood, then the particular function-oriented institutions will expand their field of activity. They will not then be conceived in isolation, as was the case with many of the projects which we viewed during the seminar. The realisation will change the scale of those institutions, and affect their change from personal exhibits to public places. The newly discovered institution will not only become part of the community, but will have the possibility of asserting itself as a new symbol of the society through a sense of belonging.

With this new institutional association the designer would have the opportunity to perform a dual responsibility: to exalt the cultural ethos through the integration of old culture with new aspirations and new technologies, and to demonstrate the most beautiful and excellent in design. In this way a seed can be sown to build affinity with the new or even with the so-called alien. The integration of such varied message experiments will have the fundamental message of honesty and truth.

I am convinced that architects and designers have much larger roles to play in the communities and societies of the future than they do today. The professional should not just be a vehicle for the expression of different attitudes, but must be, through his skill and ingenuity, a builder of attitude as well. He must be the agent who inculcates an attitude to live with others, rather than simply consolidating only the attitude to live. His designs must have a place for everybody, and must offer everyone a participatory role in the process of building the total environment. This is why I believe that architects and designers must place the highest emphasis on communal and social institutions; there is no better tool for creating an attitude for a total living environment. History has taught us this lesson, and today's growing disintegration is a result of breaking away from institutions. We must revive the institutions, we must bring them back to the forefront, and we must in due course put them back at the focal point of design if we want our communities and societies to continue advancing to the point where everybody receives a fair share of the living environment. With the equitable distribution of this share, the attitude for living together can be born. This, I believe, will result in an appropriate set of symbols and forms.

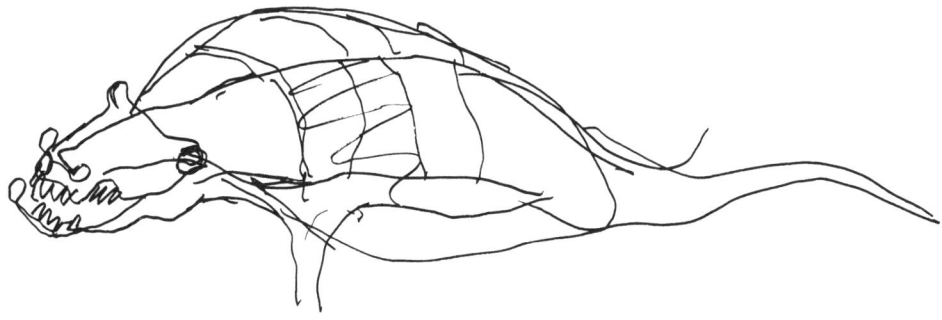

IDENTITY IN ARCHITECTURE – CONTEMPORARY PRESSURES AND TRADITION IN INDIA

1981

There are many different kinds of people in India, at many different stages of development. Some communities have grown around a particular kind of work or business, others around centres of learning or religion. Until 30 years ago, religion was not at all a separate factor. For most middle class communities, it was a philosophical force which sustained the tradition of joint family, and extending that tradition, sustained the characteristic physical pattern of both our urban and rural environments. You were always brought up in a family where there were many brothers, sisters, aunts, uncles, grandmothers and grandfathers, and sometimes, a close friend, without parents. It was not unusual for a family to include 30 or 40 members, and if you invited people for a wedding, you ended with 100 or more for dinner.

A different scale of value comes out of this kind of background, and this is the point where I really begin, the point to which my work as an architect, after years of trying and testing, is hopefully returning. The first thing on this scale of value is sharing, because you learn to respect that the other person's priorities are as important as your own. This blends with the religious attitude, the sense that you don't have to worry, that others are watching out for you just as you are watching out for them. I was brought up in this kind of family, and since my parents and relatives had come from small towns and villages, I visited such places in the summer. My affinity for village life comes from that, as does my affinity for planning principles that simulate and stimulate that kind of closeness – the narrow lanes, the quiet little courtyards in from the main streets, and the streets themselves lined with porches, actual extensions of the houses. I think that if I could go out from one of these villages every day, working on a farm, I would be very happy. Because there's a different dimension to it – not of time, not of money, but of something that is not describable, of just being happy.

My parents come from a furniture manufacturing family, so someone was always putting something together. My grandfather started a shop in 1882. The shop was below, people came in and out, some quarters were above with more people coming in and out. Our joint family was, in a sense, everyone else's joint family. There were a couple of fires in my grandfather's shop, so there were ups and downs, but this joint family really cushioned us. I could not have helped but noticed the relationship of practical needs and activities. People living and working, close to each other – that, to me, is not just an old social tradition but a permanent principle for designing new places for people to live and work.

But I did not start out to design buildings. In school, when I took classes in painting, my teacher pointed out my sense of proportion, the mathematics of my composition, and suggested that I had an aptitude for architecture. This is the reason I ended up in Bombay, at the state college. Still, I was not sure of myself. So I left the architecture course and after four years, thinking that the best way to study might be on my own.

I went to London. Its libraries were a real education, plus the people I met. By accident, I met Le Corbusier in 1950. He was in London for an architectural congress and through an acquaintance, one of his senior assistants, I got to attend the congress. What a great accident.

He was starting to design the Indian city of Chandigarh, the capital of Punjab, and so I started working in his office. I didn't know French, and being an apprentice, he wasn't supposed to pay me for eight months so I starved. I had no idea of what great architecture was, not in the immediate, exacting, personal sense of participating in its conception. I was swept into an ocean, a new world, an emptiness full of possibility and responsibility so remote from my education in Bombay, I was swept into a vacuum.

I have been swept into them recurrently, since then I don't know what happens. Every period that comes is like an increment of evolution. Every time, every day something new results. One of these moments was after taking my architectural examination. Le Corbusier had said I should have a certificate before going home. And for whatever reason, he seemed to have enjoyed the efforts I had made. On the last day, having gone through my examination, I visited his house. He showed

me his famous paintings and prints. As usual they were spread around the tables and down on the floor. 'What do you like among these?' he asked. I picked up a gouache from 1942. He said, 'You selected the one I would have selected; therefore, I want you to take one more.' I did so. He said, 'Ah, that is also good. Now take another.' Finally he gave me one which he signed, right there. I finally had a true certificate – from a great artist.

When in 1954, I was nearing my association with Le Corbusier, Sigfried Giedion, the great historian of architecture, came to the office and wanted to go out with me and talk. We did. That was it. We parted. I went home. One day a letter arrived. It had been floating around for weeks. It was from the Graham Foundation for Advanced Study in the Fine Arts. Giedion had told them that I should be invited to submit my drawings for a fellowship.

I travelled. And then another unplanned thing happened. One of my friends in New York mentioned an architect named Louis Kahn. 'Why don't we go and see his work?' We did. Lou showed us his work and looked over mine. He liked it. We became extremely close. Back home in India, a building was projected in Ahmedabad. The client asked if I would like the job. 'Why not invite Louis Kahn?' So I did. I looked after Louis's projects. He would come to India and spend the evening in my house, with my children. I miss him very much, not only as a friend but as someone I really enjoyed – as one of my family…

My architecture began with Le Corbusier. Then came a phase in which I designed buildings which, though closer to India, could really have been in any other place. These were not mine, and this phase went on for many years. Now, gradually, I am beginning to free myself. But to be free is not just a conscious act. Of course it is, in a way, but it has to be unconsciously done. You aren't just suddenly free of your earlier phases. Yet if you are not aware of what you are, then you are what you aren't. Without this awareness that allows you to move to the core of your being, you end up with an image of yourself that is a composite of images: it has been applied to you, it is not something which emanates from inside.

This is what I m trying to find out. 'How will I really become myself, so that there is a poise, a peace, that is naturally expressed in what I do?' This is what really amazed me when I went to Hindu temples in the South – the temples, yes, and the villages and the people – I saw them afresh. And now I m reading Indian things. I sit down every day for a couple of hours. Out of this has come a change in my attitude to all the relationships that compose the flow of Indian life. 'How does that self that I want to become fit in this flow? The poise, the peace – where do they reside?'

Perhaps they all reside in the realisation that there is no hurry where there is a true meaning. Though we are operating at one level the soul is eternal, so why worry about this particular moment. Between the start of what we call life, between one act and the next act, there is continuity. I stand in a village. I live in the mountains. I actually find the eternal. It is there. That realisation of myself.

So the problem of design has to do with the derivative of a pattern, for human purpose, from this flow – the extrication of a set of elements from a timeless source, the assembly of those elements to reflect the poise, the peace, the tranquility, the integrity of that flow. Consider animals, for example, A lion or a leopard or a deer or a snake. There is a fantastic poise. Is their poise conscious? Is their behaviour planned? A similar perception pertains to the buildings. How do you make a building with the poise of a deer, the tranquility of a tree? Which means, does the thing you are making reflect the realisation that each part is related to all other parts? That is the restriction on all life and all art. Interdependence is the restriction, perhaps. Realising it is finally the freedom to create.

The freedom? Yes, that point where you become clear enough to look at a situation as the source of design, not a design as something that you impose upon a situation. Yes, that point where you have learned how to become still enough to listen to that continuity which I spoke of as real.

I try to make my own buildings in such a way that, ultimately, you don't have to notice them as being dominant. What you notice is the life that goes on around them. In the case of some of my housing, people have come up to me, or called me, to say that I gave them a nice place, that they are glad. That is important. In another case, I built housing in stone, and it looks as if it had been there a long time. That is also important. I really want to find out more about making buildings that don't look like they were done today. The most difficult task has been getting out of the ego, getting free of education. I was educated outside of India, learned from the great masters, but I was still being educated outside of myself. Which is why I have tried to become a son of the soil, to go back and see what it's really like, to cast off the skin, as a snake would, to become again – and again.

I hope that my buildings will tell you whether or not my effort is succeeding. I hope they will tell you about life, about people, and about light and land. I hope that they tell you about joy. Maybe they will tell you that someone sat at a drafting board, as you might in a temple, and bent over the paper, as you might in prayer. That would be a very practical and useful kind of a building.

VOHRA HOUSES
IN GUJARAT

1984

The rhythm created by variations in vertical divisions sometimes $1 = 3 = 2 = 1\frac{1}{2}$ etc

Dawoodi Vohras are Shi'as of the Musta'lian division of Islam sect, numbering more than a million in India and abroad. As early as 765 AD, upon the death of Ja'far Sadik, the sixth Imam, dispute arose regarding the successor. Among them the majority supported Musi Kazim, the second son of Jaafar and become known as Isna-Ashari. Later, the supporters of Musi's nephew started a distinct Ismaili group in Egypt, rose to great power and flourished until 1094 AD. There are two differing beliefs regarding the origin of the Vohras in India. According to some historians, the eighteenth Imam, Al Mustansir Billah, sent his Dai-ul-Mutlaq, Maulai Ahmed to India in Hijari 467 (1047 AD) to propogate the religion in the eastern countries. The Dai landed at Khambhat, then a prosperous port town of Gujarat. He stayed here for a long time and studied the local language, culture and religion. Influenced by his wisdom, Balam Nath and Rup Nath, two Hindu boys travelled to Missr (Egypt) with him on his return journey. There they were converted to the Islamic faith and baptised as Abdullah and Nuruddin respectively; and educated to propogate Islam in India. According to another belief, during the reign of Al-Mustansir Billah, it was decided to send missionaries beyond the valley of Sindu and two eminent dais, Maulai Abdullah, were sent to India from Egypt via Yemen. Their tombs at Khambhat are visited by the Dawoodis even today as places of pilgrimage.

Maulai Abdullah subsequently settled at Khambhat, learnt the local language and acquired the knowledge about lifestyles, culture and religions of the native Hindus. In those days, a Hindu saint was the object of general faith. Opposing him was dangerous, so, Abdullah became his disciple. His wisdom impressed the saint and he was allowed to refer to holy books on Hinduism. Through his study of Hinduism, Abdullah prevailed upon the saint on religious premise, and converted him to Islam. Following this, many of the saint's followers adopted the new faith. Later, witnessing more miracles, even the ministers of the king, and the king himself adopted Islam. This accelerated the rate of conversion. As observed by Satish Misra, in his book *Muslim communities in India,* 'the first penetration of Islam in India was peaceful and the rise of this new community was imperceptible'.

It is difficult to establish correctly the actual number of early converts in Gujarat. According to Mausami-Bahar, on a single day at Patan, 260 pounds of (*janoi*) sacred threads worn by Hindus were taken off upon their embracing Islam. The number of new converts kept rising continuously for the next 250 years, until about 1380 AD.

Most of these converts were from the poor and middle class strata of the society. The democratic premise of Islam with an emphasis on equality among people had a greater appeal to the lower castes and other subcastes of the Hindus. Since Islam had originated among the prefeudal trading classes of Mecca and other desert nomads of Arabia, matured in the feudal environment of Persia, the Islamic sect imbided many a progressive element of the religious and cultural outlook of these regions. While in India, the Hindu traders were having conflicts not only with the feudal lords but also with those who were lower in the caste hierarchy, like the untouchables. As a result, the traders were more inclined to adopt Islam with its strong sense of equality.

This could be the main reason for conversions mainly among the trading castes. To transact or to trade in the local language means *vohrvu* and, people engaged in trade became to be known as Vohras, also written as Bohras. From the scrutiny of some of the social practices of this community and from *Mirat-i-Ahmadi*, a book written in the 17th century, it is found that the Brahmin and Bania traders were also converted to this new faith.

Habitat characteristics

The residential zones in traditional Indian settlements comprise distinct neighbourhoods linked by the city's thoroughfares. These neighbourhoods are characterised by an introvert organisation with an entrance gate. Religious and other community buildings, large and small open spaces for festive occasions, are located within the neighbourhood to enable a full social life within it.

Such an introverted, physical layout evolved as a response to the general insecurity in the medieval times. Amongst the Hindus these neighbourhoods were formed on the basis of castes and subcastes. This meant, that in each neighbourhood, the inhabitants would be pursuing the same occupation, as well as the social and religious practices peculiar to that subcaste or occupation. Physically, these neighbourhoods are a closed system of streets approached through a gate from the city throughfares. Two to three-storeyed houses open directly into the meandering narrow streets which widen at intervals to form spaces for the community activities and the community buildings.

It was natural for the Vohras to form their own neighbourhoods, known as a Vohrawad, in such a context. Distinct Vohrawads were observed in all the settlements visited for this study in the Gujarat state.

The Vohras are a minority community in India and the need for security is strongly felt by them. Their sociocultural and religious practices also demand the location of their houses in the close vicinity of their priest's residence, the mosque and the community hall. As most of them are traders, and frequently travel to other towns for business, they prefer that their family members should stay amongst members of their community. All these factors gave rise to the Vohrawad as a distinct sector of a town. It was observed during the study that the Vohrawads from different settlements fall in two categories based on their physical layout.

One, an organic development characteristic of the traditional city pattern and, the other, a gridiron layout based on the right angle geometry. However, both the developments still maintain a closed system of streets, sub-streets and small open spaces accessible only through a gate linking the city thoroughfares and the overall urban fabric.

Almost all the Vohrawads, which are more than 100 years old, evolved organically within the confines of the available land in the fortified city.

In the second half of the 19th century, the Britishers consolidated their hold in India and a relatively peaceful environment prevailed. The Vohras contract with Britishers, and exposure through travel abroad, must have led to the creation of the second category of Vohrawads. These newer Vohrawads generally occur adjacent to an old Vohrawad on the fringe of the settlements. Not constrained by the shape and size of the land, Vohras could lay out these clusters in a gridiron pattern.

The main buildings include: a mosque, the assembly hall for religious discourses, the local priests' house, a travellers' lodge and community hall for ceremonial occasions especially the commensurate dinners on various occasions such as the birthday of the local priest, the first ten days of Mahorram or the anniversary of a saint etc.

The House

A typical Vohra house is distinguished by its facade decoration, the treatment of the openings and rich materials of construction. Apart from a typical space use pattern discriminating between the private and semi-public domain, the basic plan of a Vohra house is found very much similar to that of a Hindu house which, conforms to the general pattern of a medieval town with houses in a row, sharing two walls with the adjoining units. In a Vohra dwelling the typical space organisation is described below.

At the ground level one enters the house through a portico raised about 75cm above street level. Through the main door, one steps into an anteroom, known as a *delhi* separated by a light screen from the inner court to ensure privacy inside the house. This space usually houses a stair which directly leads to the upper floors. Visitors are directly led up to the formal sitting room on the first floor from here. Next the open to sky court houses all the services on its side walls.

The space immediately after the court is fully open on the court side and is referred to as *baharni parsal,* meaning external portico. This is followed by a room known as *andarni parsal,* meaning internal portico. Such a seemingly incongruous

designation of these spaces is with reference to last room of the house known as *ordo* which is the sanctum of the Vohra family's life.

For all practical purposes on the ground floor, the Vohra family only uses the spaces which are after the inner court. And, with this as a reference, the space immediately following the court becomes an external portico, followed by an inner portico and then the family room – ordo.

The upper floors are normally organised as independent rooms on either side of the court around which the services are located. In case of a house with more than one upper floors, the stair is also found to be located in the area around the court. This space is known as *ravas*. On the top floor, the *ravas* area becomes a terrace seperating the rooms in the front and at the back. A double lean-to roof over both these rooms allows an attic space underneath which is known as *daglo*. Contrary to the other communities, the Vohras rarely use the raised, street-side portico. While it is used extensively by other communities for various activities, like elders to while away their time and the children to play, the Vohras desist from this. This may be due to greater confinement of the women folk in the social set-up of Vohras.

Once inside, the anteroom serves as the second buffer between the inner domain and external domain. Generally light wooden screens are placed to avoid a clear view into the house from the street. This also serves as a brief meeting point between the men folk and the casual visitors. The staircase to the first floor is located here which directly leads the guests to the first floor sitting room. On the ground floor, beyond the anteroom, is the family domain into which only the close relatives and family friends are invited.

Open to sky court situated next helps ventilate the whole house besides letting in light on all floors. The kitchen and other services are located around the court. The court as well as the baharni parsal are used for dining and lounging. All domestic activities are also carried out here. *Bethak,* a large wooden platform with storage underneath and a soft cushion on the top is a dominant piece of furniture in this space. The family's elders while away their time here in the midst of the domestic activities. These spaces are actually the hub of the family world and used throughout the day. Next, the andarni parsal, being covered, extends this use in monsoon when the court is unusable.

The andarni parsal often has a swing which is a popular device in hot climates to keep cool. This space is used predominantly as a family lounging space during the hot afternoons. Beyond the andarni parsal, the house ends in a room, which is the family's living room. Known as ordo, this room is richly decorated with seating arrangements in traditional style on the floor. The cupboard on the extreme rear wall of this 'room' is always designed in Islamic traditions representing the concept of nine squares known as *navkhand*. Such a cupboard with intricate carvings is an inseparable component of a Dawoodi's house. This space is generally used to entertain close relatives and family friends and for sleeping.

Generally a service lane separates the next parallel row of houses. This barely ensures ventilation. The level of natural illumination is extremely low in this room on the ground floor. In case of a house with a backyard, the light in the room is satisfactory.

The first floor is reached by a stair from the anteroom at ground floor. From the first floor upwards, the stair is often provided near the court, allowing for an independent use of the rooms on its either side. A large room at the back on this level is generally used as a formal living area and guests are entertained here. The windows generally have double shutters, one of wood and the other of stained glass. The room in the front is generally used as a multipurpose space and sometimes has a covered balcony.

It is in the facades that the Vohra houses built early this century largely differ from the Hindu houses as well as in those of the initial converts. In these facades variations of European styles are dominant.

The first converts continued to occupy the Hindu houses with marginal changes within, hardly affecting the facades. As their trade flourished their dwellings and particularly the facade manifested their prosperity. At that stage, the model available for the Vohras was the dwellings of rich Hindus. Predominant use of wood and finely carved elements of facades, columns, brackets, railings, window frames etc, can be observed in the house more than 150 years old at Surat, Kapadvanj, and for example, in the case of Rupwala House at Ahmedabad, where the decoration is very much Hindu.

However, this only helped the Vohras to distinguish themselves from the poorer households but not as a community following a different religion; being a minority community, an urge for such manifestation must have been very strong for them.

Discovery of European and British facade treatment during their travels abroad, as well as in the colonial architecture in India, provided them an opportunity to further distinguish their dwellings from the rich Hindus in the region and, the Vohras adopted it en masse. By the mid 19th century, the Britishers had consolidated their political and economic hold over large parts of India, and as partners in trade, Vohras identified themselves with the Britishers and broke the Hindu roots of their habitat. Eclectic adoption of various European styles of facades at the new Vohrawad, Siddhpur, built between the 1890s and the 1930s, is clear evidence of this process. It was learnt during the survey for this study, that they even had Britishers advising them during the design and construction of these houses. This probably affected the choice of material which is no longer wood, but brick masonry with stucco.

In conclusion, our study shows that the Vohra houses have naturally evolved in the context of the region and its traditional habitat pattern. Being Hindu converts, this evolution appears to have been a slow process of modifying the space organisation and objects, and elements of daily use within the social values and religious beliefs of their new religion.

This process of evolution has been more of an additive nature, particularly in the basic plan of the house and the arrangement of the decoration and elements of interior spaces and furniture which acquired sophistication in design and detailing. This is easily noticeable in the later day house facades, furniture and fixtures, treatment of openings, internal partitions and false ceilings. This superimposition of external and internal changes on the basic plan can be attributed to the British influence on the Vohra community due to their trade relationship and an exposure to the British lifestyle in Europe.

In the planning of the neighbourhoods the introverted, security-conscious make-up of the Vohra community and its Hindu origin are explicitly manifested. Unlike the British colonial neighbourhoods, one house per a large plot on the outskirts of existing medieval towns in India, the Vohras always built houses in close-knit clusters in a row house system. These were often physically integrated with the existing random patterns of the old Vohra neighbourhoods to obtain a socio-economic interdependence and the social security. The Vohra neighbourhood is found to be similar to Hindu ones rather than the British, indicating the lack of any major change in their outlook to life and living. It is also an indication that the British influence was perhaps superficial.

For example, due to their exposure to the outside world Vohras laid new residential development on a rectilinear basis. In a few instances the row houses even had controlled street facades. With the exception of few erstwhile princely rulers who planned their towns on European models, these Vohrawards were then the only neighbourhoods in Gujarat laid out geometrically.

The British house was large in size and its verandahs adjoining the peripheral rooms opened towards the garden. The Vohra or the Hindu house on the other hand was inward looking, towards the small internal court. They had limited external openings confined by the two thick party walls.

By and large, independent use of several rooms is possible in case of the colonial house, whereas in the Vohra houses, similar to the Hindu house, all rooms occur along a single axis of movement, leaving only the last room free of the general movement which can be used without disturbance. This indicates the low priority given to a degree of privacy within the family, unlike the colonial house. Since privacy vis-à-vis outsiders is of greater concern to Vohras than Hindus. And this is indicated by a screen between the internal court and anteroom, from where the visitors are directly led upstairs to the formal sitting room. Apart from these minor, localised additions, the basic plan organisation remains the same as its Hindu origins.

Even when opportunities were available, as in the case of the house of Taherbhai Madraswala at Siddhpur, there is no effort at evolving a more sophisticated plan organisation in spite of its larger width and location facilitating three open sides. As a result even such a large house becomes 'twice' the traditional house. It appears that the strong colonial influence is only manifested in the decoration of the interiors and the furniture for the purpose of identity only to express their contact with the external world, which dealt in business and economic status. Yet, basically the inner beings of the Vohras remained the same.

As observed in the chart, the Hindus and the Vohras, being situated in the congested old city fabric, had to build houses with several storeys to meet the area requirements. For light and ventilation, these houses employed an open to sky court through all the floors, similar to old Hindu houses. On the other hand, the Britishers spread their houses on the vast plot available to them and eliminated the internal courtyards. However, there are examples of colonial houses where, by differing the ceiling heights, better ventilation and light have been achieved to satisfy the need for greater ventilaion in a hot humid climate.

It can be said that over the centuries Vohras have definitely evolved a house character which is largely distinct from that of other houses in the region. The space-use pattern, the treatment of the facades and the decorations are characteristically different from a Hindu house. Vohras, in their search for a separate identity, judiciously utilised elements of European architecture via the British influence. However, the influences have only been skin deep. No radical changes took place in the Vohras' social values and religious beliefs and this is reflected in their habitat which basically remains very much the same as the Hindu one of their origin, reflecting the strong adherence to their traditional way of life and thought.

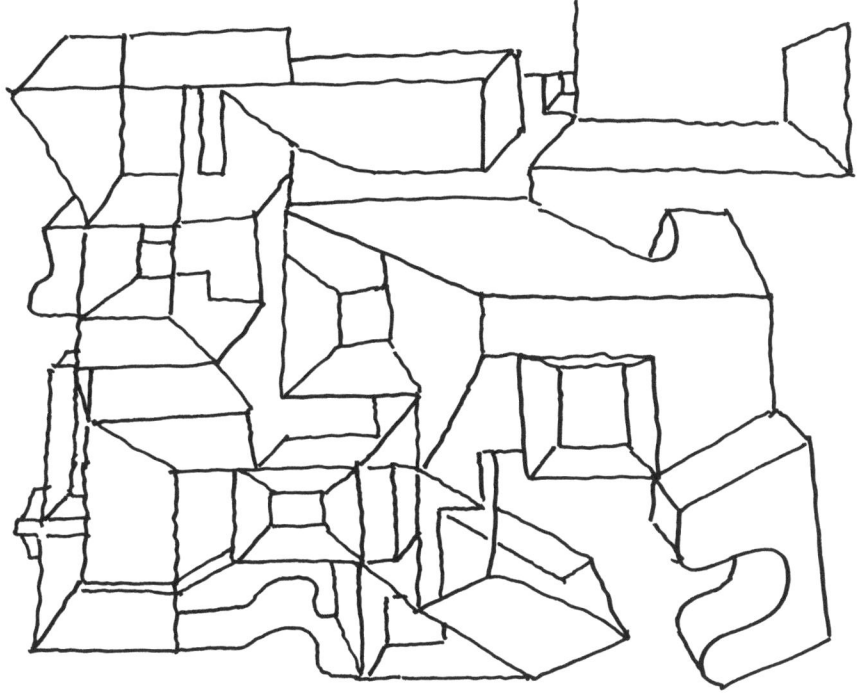

CULTURAL CONTINUUM AND REGIONAL IDENTITY IN ARCHITECTURE

1985

Introduction

The last few years have rightly witnessed a growing debate among the developing countries, particularly those which experienced intense colonisation, about the state of architectural design and planning practices. The realisation that Western models of architecture and urban planning introduced by the colonising agencies, as well as the subsequent developments in the West, were not very suitable to their own resources and climatic circumstances and sociocultural well-being has led to a lot of healthy questioning. This has also required them to look into their own past heritage to understand the architectural and planning practices which evolved over centuries of adaptation and in a few cases adoption.

The theme of this seminar, some of the recent publications like MIMAR, and a shifting emphasis in research areas among academics, are indicative of a very subtle beginning in an extremely crucial aspect of built-environment design, that of seeking beyond mere visual aspirations dominated by and large by the International Modern Movement, and exploring the abstract, cultural undercurrents which nourish society, using the built environment in its dual cause and effect role.

This paper discusses two major parameters of this role of the built environment. It begins by dealing with more tangible issues, reviewing current design practices vis-à-vis the traditions and resource situation in India. Later it deals with the intangible parameters, which seek to explain built form as a manifestation of sociocultural institutions which are looked into as a dynamic relationship nurturing and complementing each other.

Search for a 'postmodern' regional architecture

Pre-industrial architecture of any given region had the strength to serve the physical and spiritual needs of people, from a single family to the entire community. At the physical level, it embodied centuries of learning with regard to orientation, climate, building materials and construction techniques. At the spiritual level, the built form conveyed total harmony with the lifestyle in all its daily as well as seasonal rituals, unifying the sociocultural and religious aspirations of the individuals and the community.

To achieve this unity and to integrate physical and spiritual needs, due importance was given to nature and its basic laws. Nature was accepted as it is. Lifestyle and activity followed in consonance with nature and architecture with nature. Concern for resources and conservation of energy was reflected in all rituals, social actions and very clearly in physical planning.

The compactness of the town plan, building using thick walls with niches, and a variety of in-between elements like balconies, incorporated both the symbolic as well as social meaning. Jaisalmer, Old Jaipur and Old Delhi are testimonies to such thinking. The application of such realistic, and yet value-oriented attitudes, gave society a sense of confidence and a much needed feeling of self-sufficiency. External considerations were accepted under duress and were gradually absorbed to facilitate the continuance of the envisaged lifestyle. The transformation of the Mughal architecture to suit India is a case in point. In this process, the role played by everyone including the architect was that of shareholder in an enterprise. While the roles of each discipline may be demarcated, the final outcome expressed the multiple considerations that went into making it. That is how all different forms of art in India have, over the centuries, given birth to a vernacular idiom, sustained the culture and in the process, sustained itself.

The transformation

Unfortunately, during the last two centuries, our concepts and lifestyles have undergone considerable changes. Initially, it was the internal strife, then the foreign rule, then the destruction of small-scale home-based crafts which affected the nature of the social pattern. Subsequent emphasis on industrialisation, the advent of new building materials, and a desire to 'modernise' gave rise to different patterns of building and community-city planning. The models for such development were neither conceived on the basis of our climate, nor social needs, nor lifestyle, nor did they incorporate the attributes of the process mentioned earlier. The consequence was an increased use of resources, of energy and subsequent degradation of the environment.

Today, our situation is even worse. We have a large and growing population below subsistency level, the natural resources are depleting, the forest cover is being used as fuel and the metropolitan cities are expanding. Our physical environment is desolate, without trees, with isolated 'modern' buildings surrounded by slums and pollution is on the increase. Another disturbing factor is the high technology-oriented industry in the metropolis and the neglect of cottage industry in the rural area. The rural-urban harmony and interdependence is broken in this process.

All this is occurring in the villages, towns and cities, which have a rich cultural heritage. What we constantly realise is the apparent contradiction between what we had and what we have now. Thus, we live in an atmosphere of contradictions because we like what we had, but do not yet know well how to improve the present and ensure a better future. As a result we attempt, superficially, certain measures in town and city planning, house designs and housing layouts. The cultural heritage does not appeal to the heart of the younger generations, they do not wish to retain it since it does not symbolically or culturally belong to them. They look towards the new world which they witness through the ever-expanding communication media. The young generation's image is that of the outside world, because they do not have any clue of our own heritage.

The confusion we face today

Since Independence, either due to an urge to keep up with a rapidly modernising economy, or lacking a societal concern, the profession has followed a different path. As against the traditional solutions which responded to the local resources and climate, the designer has opted for techniques and forms propagated by the new technology. The hot, impersonal beehives of flats, in concrete, in isolated locations, separated by unsuitable public spaces, have led to social disintegration and environmental degradation. In settlement planning similar things followed. As against mixed land-use which promoted economies of various types, the single function zones were created. This not only wasted space but also added strain on energy in transportation of goods and people.

This situation, coupled with an irrelevant academic curriculum, and lack of professional leadership, developed a breed of professionals whose main interests revolved around the estate developers' needs. Social responsibility and cultural values were too dangerous to seek for fear of losing the commission. Because of tempting commissions to build for an elite group which responds to an alien 'modernity', the professionals and the academic institutions failed to advocate the achievements and the essential order of the dynamic design process of the past. In the absence of this, a formal character of design was repeated without hesitation as the only solution.

The cultural shock is even greater. It even makes the uninitiated question the basis of earlier lifestyles and the worth of past architecture and city planning practices. The conflict is between the 'old' which was one's own and the 'new', which though alien, is apparently impressive.

A case in hand, at national level, is our more than half a million villagers with about 580 million population. Even today, after 38 years of independence, our rural economy is faced with the problems of shortages in food, clothing, shelter, and educational and health facilities. This is the result of our initial emphasis on heavy industries and not on developing small and medium towns as integrated communities providing opportunities for a wholesome life.

We have today extremes of development without proper links. We have sophisticated technology including the atomic power plants and jet air transportation on the one hand, and bullock cart on the other. A few cities are becoming

Feb 78 5/2/78

overpopulated with the concentration of industries, and the smaller towns and villages are becoming depopulated due to a lack of basic needs and work opportunities. In such a state of unbalanced development, what should the priorities of architecture and planning be? What is the so-called 'true' architecture? Which end of the stick should we grasp first?

Such a state of affairs, once it has set in, is difficult to correct. In such a situation, the technologies for production of basic needs are in great demand. The mass media, radio, television and films, have brought to the mostly uneducated population an awareness of the life in developed countries. As a consequence, the growing number of people dependent on a limited developed land area aspire for a new world; a world of plenty and comforts. New gadgets that are seen through the mass media become a fascination. The choice open to them is to search for a place where the happiness of their dream can be realised. The reaction naturally is to move to a better place. Thus movement from less developed to developed places takes place. No one is able to control this exodus.

The emerging issues

We note that this situation is an unavoidable consequence of industrialisation. What solution do we have for either the urban or the rural areas? Since the technological benefits should be given to the masses, irrespective of their location, what are we, as architects and planners, doing? Are we really developing a technology for orderly and contented living conditions for many, or are we generating through education and planning some ways of helping the rural population to have a better place or well-conceived industrial activities for lean periods, or better tools for farming?

In such situations, what kind of role can be expected from architecture and community planning? Since the entire development has depended on uncontrolled circumstances and has discounted 'man', what style of buildings can we expect?

What can be taught to the coming generations? What professional services can we offer? Where do we really begin?

The effects of such uncoordinated development has had more disastrous effects in developing countries than in the developed countries. For where can the poor nations find additional resources to rectify its ever-growing mistakes of blind imitation?

The Indian cultural heritage and community environment

Over the centuries, Indian culture, through its socio-economic ramifications, has given a sense of security and yet allowed wide choices. In the traditional Indian society, one is not alone, but part of a community. Buildings are not built in isolation, but in groups leading to a total environment, merging buildings, spaces and culture in a unified whole. The community shares everything, be it an economic activity or a festival. Unless this sociocultural tradition is understood, the organisation of buildings, streets, spaces and their forms cannot be the desired fabric wherein the community wants to live. It is, therefore, necessary to talk about physical environment in terms of culture rather than only in terms of buildings, space, technology or economy.

The house form which has evolved in India, say in Ahmedabad, can be cited as an example. This form has behind it centuries of tradition, which not only ties the community of one generation together, but also the successive generations within the house. In the house plans, it is difficult to perceive this immediately, but seen through the minute activities and functions carried out in the house, it can be felt that there exists a strong sense of identity. This must be incorporated in designing new environments and, to do this, it is necessary to understand the sociocultural patterns.

The illustration of a simple village well, as an element representing a sociocultural pattern, has often been quoted. The water well is an institution which binds the community very strongly because this is where people meet each other daily, discuss their problems, find solace in their griefs, and feel socially cared for. The village well over centuries has grown as a very prominent social institution. There are a large number of such manifestations in the old and existing institutions which tell us about the sociocultural tradition of the community. Detailed study of these can provide us with a genuine understanding of the real community needs, which must be given importance in architecture and design.

Therefore, institutions became the primary design elements in creating an environment. Religious institutions particularly the temple, through the ages have greatly influenced the community environment. There are temple cities in India which have survived for centuries because the religious institutions have provided the community with cultural stability, occupation and guidance in its behavioural patterns. These also helped in establishing value systems and a strong conviction in continuous community belonging.

For the institutions to survive, grow, expand and be a part of the culture, there was an organisational structure evolved by the society. In the Ajanta and Ellora caves, while the building activity continued over centuries, the quality of execution and the craftsmanship continued to grow better. Today, the work assigned to an assistant or to a contractor cannot achieve the expected quality if the designer is absent for even a few months. In the case of these caves and temples, the chief architect or the 'sthapati' would come, spend some time and then go away. He perhaps would not come again, but the work went on through generations, with the quality remaining constant and often improving. This process had within it the built-in mechanism of community commitment and convictions passed down through generations. The generations of designers, builders and craftsmen would continue to build the institution, each excelling the previous one, motivated by their commitment to remain true to the major principles, and guidelines, established by the sthapati with regard to the location, the materials, the technology, the design of the carvings and the sense of depth. This suggests that within a main concept, an organisational system and a method must be developed to continue the work, to provide choice for participants to identify themselves with the work and thus generate excellence. This quality of transition, of commitment to the community, and the ability and sanction to interpret principles by individuals are very much in contrast to contemporary practices. There, perhaps, greater importance is given to the individual and his role, and not to the organisation. People today presumably believe that when the individual dies, the organisation also comes to an end.

It is interesting to see therefore why Indian culture has survived through many centuries and why it is good in some ways. This is because, through centuries, institutions have evolved along with the living environment and provided a broad flexible structure which an individual has the 'choice' to interpret in his own way. As a result, the commitment to the concept of community has been deep-rooted and this has tended to provide for total harmony. The built-in variations in all aspects of Indian life, and activity creation always provide an 'open end' with regard to growth, evolution and change. This is another very important aspect to remember. In our modern attitude to development planning, building and designing, these issues, though basic, are often ignored when preconceived or alien strategies do not work and hence planning and designing becomes totally inefficient.

Such attitudes to organisation, structure and design can be discovered in past Indian architecture, particularly that of the temples which have served as the most important catalytic institutions to preserve the culture. In Indian architecture, the creators, the designers, thought about many functions other than just simply the basic functions the buildings should perform. The idea of a staircase performing only the function of movement, a window that of lighting and ventilation, or a roof that of providing shelter from the weather, are basically alien to Indian culture since such cannot satisfy the diverse needs of diverse groups. A staircase can mean many things, a place to sit, or if bigger, perhaps a place to sleep.

All elements were considered as multifunctional. That is what Indian culture has grown with, and that is how the Indian temperament is built. Growth of buildings are not just additive but are basic to the balanced life. Therefore, all elements of the environment must be designed to satisfy more than one situation.

This reminds me of one of Charles Eames' descriptions of a 'lota', the traditional vessel for fetching water, and also a conversation recorded in *Vishnudharmottar Purana,* a 12th century treatise of arts. In the example of the lota, Charles Eames, with his highly developed sense, saw in it the total process of not only its making, its form or its use as a container, but also in it the users' various postures when carrying it from the well or the river, on the head or on the waist or in the hand. He also heard in it the sound of water, and therefore, regarded the form of the lota as a demonstration of one of the most essential processes of design which is neither time nor space bound. How its design came about or who the designer was is not clearly known. The fact that it has so many attributes gives it a place in the history of design.

In the other example from *Vishnudharmottar Purana,* the King asks Lord Markendeya how to build a shrine for Him so that the Lord is available for daily worship. In His reply, the Lord explains to the King, the process of design and how to learn this process. Here, phonetics, poetry, literature, art, music, painting and sculpture are mentioned as basic and successive tools of learning without which a designer cannot fulfil his task of building a temple cohesively related to the symbolic and functional aspects. It is apparent from the above that a good design must include several tangible and intangible functions: what Louis Kahn called the measurables and the unmeasurables, the physical and the spiritual or the symbolic.

Directions for the future – the possibilities

With today's technologies, it should be easy to build a new world, a world which can be linked with the past by building on the basic values, and with the future in terms of the well-being of a larger number of people. Planning will only succeed, provided uncertainties about 'values' are reduced to a minimum and not subject to pressures of immediate circumstances.

Fortunately, we are becoming aware of the consequence of our present day actions and we are dissatisfied. We realise that it is necessary to accept technological advances and explorations of new avenues for growth. It is of great importance to harness resources and energies to support the ever-increasing population. What we have not perhaps understood properly is a place for the technology. It is really a tool but the tool has become a hammer which we can't wield. Technology is not an end in itself. Unbridled technology can lead to overproduction resulting in wasteful consumption. Essentially, technology should be utilised in relation to man's welfare.

Our main aim should be to become industrious not merely industrialised. By becoming industrious, that is, through skill and healthy competition and choice, we can have a better rapport between work that one enjoys doing and leisure as its counterpoint. Our approach should be based on using life, time and space more fruitfully. With this the problem of quantity, that is, the need of the large number of people, will be interlinked with quality. This will improve the values since quality will convert the quantity into an expression of life's desire and will not belong to the realm of competition, because, it will not be superfluous but inherently essential.

To this end, what sort of planning and architecture is most helpful? What considerations should the professionals have, so that its expressions have a bearing on the history and the culture of the people? Should our architectural and community planning focus on social expectations, religious faith, aesthetic outlook, or only an economic affluence? It is accepted that we as professionals, with a limited field of control, cannot directly provide for the amelioration of economic conditions. We may however be able to decide on courses through which economic growth not only becomes possible but progressive. This we can do. On the other hand, we may not be able to change the social customs and manners of a people, but we can plan in a manner that provides for a healthy accommodation of these. The architect-planner naturally cannot preach any religious doctrine, but whatever the religious form, he can plan and provide for the individual or for the community, choices for prayers, for meditation, for ceremonies or for festivals.

In terms of operation and management for balanced growth, we need to discover scales which are self-sufficient in certain respects and, at the same time, interdependent for certain operations.

We should define, at least to a close approximation, the scales of various operations for an individual, family and community in villages, towns and cities so that their mode of living is in relation not only to a cycle of 24 hours but also in relation to weekly, monthly and annual needs. In this way every individual, who ultimately constitutes the community and the city, has his own choices for work, rest, reflection and creation.

Quality will naturally emerge in time, provided the entire process is nurtured with this faith. This should be the basis of planning or architecture. This is what we call culture, and the structure around which people like to throng are the 'institutions of man'. We should search for our cultural 'catalysts' which become the institutions of man and which give life its meaning. In planning practices and in architectural expressions, this is what we have to look for and build.

LEARNING FROM OLD JAIPUR

BY BALKRISHNA DOSHI & MUKTIRAJSINHJI CHAUHAN

1987

The walled city of Jaipur strongly represents an approach to planning concerns at all seals of the habitat, which is assured of a timeless quality. Perhaps the right solution for all times to come for the region.

Concerns for optimal use of man and material resources, an urban fabric which is energy conscious, flexibility and growth within an overall framework, harmonious urbanism and a humane pedestrian scale are achievements of this city worthy of emulating with humility and necessary reinterpretation for contemporary needs.

Learning from Old Jaipur

Vidyadhar Nagar is conceived as a reflection of its parent city, Jaipur. Jaipur, the city, which invokes popularity amongst scholars as well as laymen.

Its unique conception, execution and that it is still a thriving well-preserved city after 258 years, makes it an excellent example for understanding the architectural and planning traditions in our contexts.

Planning for Vidyadhar Nagar in the proximity of such an environment becomes a challenging task aimed at judiciously combining the lessons from the traditions to the contemporary era. Added to this challenge is the role Vidyadhar Nagar is expected to play in the fast-developing north-western sector of the Jaipur city. Like Old Jaipur which functions as the hub of activities for the subsequent developments to its south, Vidyadhar Nagar is expected to play a similar role in the south-western sector. In built environmental terms, this implies that besides the activity dependence, the urban 'character' of Vidyadhar Nagar must attain a quality which the inhabitants as well as daily and occasional visitors can be proud of. Being named after the architect planner of Old Jaipur, Vidyadhar Nagar should be a fitting tribute to the ingenuity of Vidyadhar Bhattacharya, whose visionary plan integrating basic elements of planning with philosophical value-oriented lifestyles is valid even today.

With this aim, the planning team has undertaken several studies of Old Jaipur at varying scales of habitat. The emphasis in these studies has been to understand planning and architecture of the old city.

Historical Background

King Sawai Jai Singh (1700–1743), the founder of Jaipur, ascended the throne of Amber (situated about 8km north of Old Jaipur) at the age of 13. Using a judicious mixture of stratagem and statesmanship he brought prosperity to his kingdom through strong links with the Mughal emperor Aurangzeb and control over the local, smaller principalities.

In these prosperous and peaceful circumstances, it was but natural that he would want a new capital city. Amber, dating back to the 10th century, was sited on a hilly terrain with a strong fortification to meet the demands of a kingdom in process of establishing itself. Its site precluded the potential for expansion necessitated by the prosperous conditions of the early 18th century. Being a learned man, well-versed in many fields of sciences and arts, Sawai Jai Singh would naturally aspire that his capital reflect his wider consciousness. This might have strengthened his desire for a new capital city.

He was ably assisted for fulfilling this ambition by his architect, Vidyadhar Bhattacharya, great grandson of the priest of the king's temple at Amber. Vidyadhar had successfully undertaken construction of important structures for the king before the founding of the city on 17 November 1727.

Besides Vidyadhar's skills, Jai Singh's pursuit of astronomy, arts and particularly the study of ancient scriptures seemed to be the major inspiration behind the conception of the plan of Old Jaipur. His interest in astronomy was exhaustive, and he had obtained a thorough knowledge of its principles. He was fully familiar with astronomical methods of Hindus, Muslims and Europeans and seemed to have closely followed the Muslim astronomer Ulugh Beg. His library included works like Ptolemy's *Almagest,* which he had his assistant translate into Sanskrit from Arabic. Finding the ancient astronomical tables defective, he took up the task of preparing new ones. For the purpose of gathering new observations, he set up a series of observatories in five cities: Benares, Mathura, Ujjain, Delhi and Jaipur. Besides his interest in astronomy, Jai Singh was thoroughly familiar with Hindu scriptures, particularly related to Vastu Shastra and fine arts. It is natural that when such a scholarly sensitive king decided to build for himself a new capital city, his vision would be equally expansive in conception.

Records indicate that Jai Singh took special care to invite groups of various traders and craftsmen to assure success for the new city he was founding. Being conscious of the social and economic interdependence and the hierarchy prevalent in a tradition-bound society, Jai Singh planned different zones of the city in conformity with the Vastu Shastra. Brahmins thus were allocated areas in the north, Kshatriyas in east, Vaishyas in south and the Sudras (artisans) in the west. This arrangement, as can be observed, strengthened the economic base of Jaipur. The major roads, which were designed along with commercial facilities by the state, were the first structures to be constructed in the new city.

The concepts and its application

Many scholars have attributed the very basic concept plan of Old Jaipur as being a *Prastara* a typed mentioned in *Mansara,* one of the ancient treatises on Hindu town planning. The physical interpretation of the basic Prastara scheme in the final plan of Old Jaipur is obvious.

British historian, George Mitchell has observed that any study of cities and symbolism in Asia must inevitably focus on Jaipur. According to him, it is not only the best preserved example in India of a town laid out according to traditional Hindu theory, but it embodies ideas that may have travelled to India by way of the Islamic invasion and which are pre-Islamic in origin.

These ideas are concerned with linking the city with the heavens, either by recreating the structure of the universe in the form of a sacred mandala or by incorporating it into the city, the means by which the heavens may be observed and movement of stars measured. Interestingly, the central position in a mandala is occupied by Brahma, which could be readily interpreted as the position of the king in the case of monarchy. While at Jaipur, locating both the palace complex and an observatory to study the heavens, Brahmand further strengthens the symbolic case sought to be made of recreating a city in the image of the universe.

George Mitchell cites the example of a town, Koy-Krylgan Kala Khwarazm (now in the USSR), built in 400 BC in what he calls near-eastern tradition. This town was essentially an observatory city. According to Mitchell, even though this region was linked to India through trade, a stronger link for an exchange of ideas must have existed. The fact being that in the 15th century, Ulugh Beg's observatory at Samarquand in Transoxiana was situated close to Khwarazm. As we already know, Jai Singh was well-acquainted with the work of Ulugh Beg and presumably the concept of an observatory city might have influenced him greatly. This was further strengthened by his desire to create a city symbolically expressive of the universe through a mandala and according to the ancient Indian tenets of town planning.

Vastu Purusha Mandala
According to ancient texts, a long time ago something existed that was not defined by name or known in its form. It blocked the sky and the earth. When the gods saw it they seized it and pressed it upon the ground, face downward. Brahma had it occupied by the gods to hold it down and called it 'Vastu Purusha'. Thus an existence which did not follow any principle is defined by Brahma who forces it to assume and retain a certain mandala form with the aid of gods presiding over it.

With the central location presided by Brahma, the inner and outer rings of the mandala were occupied by 44 other Vedic gods. In Indian symbolism, a square represents a celestial world and with the gods appropriately sited over the mandala, eg sun god to east, the Vastu Purusha Mandala assumes great significance to town planning and architecture.

'The Vastu Purusha Mandala is an image of the laws governing the cosmos, to which men are just as subject as in the earth in which they build. In their activity as builders, men order their environment in the same way as once in the past Brahma forced the undefined *purusha* into a geometric form. For the architect, building is an act of bringing disordered existence into conformity with basic laws that govern it. This can only be achieved by making each monument, from the hermit's retreat to the layout of a city, follow exactly the magic diagram of the Vastu Purusha Mandala.' (Andreas Volwahsen, *Living Architecture: Indian,* 1969.)

Prastara
Mansara's description of Prastara plan is noted by Prabhakar Begde as a town, which is either square or oblong in form. It is so divided as to form the mystic figures of Paramasayika Mandala or Manduka Mandala. Paramasayika and Manduka Mandalas are the most commonly adopted divisions of the basic mandala square. These divisions number 81 in Paramasayika and 64 in the case of Manduka. Within the boundaries of the Vastu Purusha Mandala, a Prastara town is divided into four, nine or 16 major wards by an appropriate number of roads, which run east-west and north-south. Within the wards, roads are again planned on a chessboard pattern and the spacing of the roads is determined by the sizes of plots in the subdivisions. Wards with larger plots are inhabited by people of higher ranks, while the wards with smaller plots are inhabited by people of lower ranks.

Almost all published material on ancient Indian town-planning refers to the distribution of the different castes-classes within the overall framework of the Vastu Purusha Mandala by assigning them specific quarters with respect to the cardinal points. Locating the seat of religious or political power at the centre is commonly accepted. Analysis of the walled city of Jaipur suggests that the Prastara concepts for a town plan as described in *Mansara* has been adopted and further evolved in the planning of the city.

Siting

The site of Old Jaipur is in the valley formed by hills to the north and east. The old capital of Jai Singh, Amber, was located in the northern hills overlooking the valley. The southern boundary must have been determined by the ancient trade route Delhi-Agra-Ajmer, which was also used by the Mughal emperors for their pilgrimage.

Alternately, it has been speculated that the basic Prastara plan was adopted for a system of nine squares (residential sectors) or six of them as an orthogonal cluster. The presence of a single major east-west road would naturally imply a six-square version. However, the most commonly accepted interpretation of the Prastara plan is the sequence postulated by Kulbhushan Jain, which envisages an orthogonal cluster of nine squares with two major roads running east-west and north-south. Constrained by the southern boundary of the Agra-Ajmer Road, the north-western square of this orthogonal cluster of nine squares would have fallen off the hill of Nahargarh. This square, therefore, was placed adjoining the south-eastern sector. The central square in addition to the observatory accommodated the palace and its gardens, administrative offices, etc, which required a larger area and hence was merged with the square on its north.

Thus, of the two major east-west roads required for the perfect nine square cluster, only one remained. Several scholars have mentioned that a ridge ran east-west at the site and the major road came to be situated along the ridge, which also established a direct axial link to the ancient sun temple of Galtaji in the eastern hill range. This axis occurs at a 15-degree deviation to the cardinal directions, having several advantages. The significant ones being a) Persons moving in the morning and evening hours do not face the low angle sun directly; b) It allows the early morning sun in winter which is welcome and rightly avoids the evening sun in summer on buildings; and c) The angle is conducive to the predominant wind direction for flushing the streets.

It may however be noted, based on our detailed studies, that a 30 to 35-degree clockwise deviation from the cardinal direction at Jaipur allows maximum advantages for the above planning consideration in an orthogonal urban fabric. This might have been known by the king and his architect, but use of the ridge occurring along the middle of the site to facilitate the surface drainage must have been a major consideration.

Essentially the city's structure could be described as a gridiron resulting from the orthogonal clustering of square sectors along Prastara pattern. The major east-west road from Surajpol to Chandpol, and three north-west roads divide the city into eight district sectors (known as *'chowkris'*). One of them, where the palace precincts, including administrative offices and the observatory occur, is twice the average sector area. Tie sector to the south of the place was divided by introducing a north-south road in the late 19th century.

Road Network

The road network at Jaipur is well thought out and follows definite hierarchy. The major east-west, Surajpol-Chandpol road and the north-south roads which form the sector boundaries could be termed as *Rajmarg* since all of them lead to gates in the fort walls in conformity with the Prastara norms. These roads measure 33m wide. Next, there is the network of 16.5m wide which run north-south in each sector linking the internal areas of the sectors to the major activity spine formed by the Surajpol-Chandpol road. An orthogonal grid of a 8.25m and 4m road in the true Prastara chessboard pattern further divides sectors into *mohallas*, the smaller residential clusters.

The frequency of sub-sector roads is observed to reflect the individual plot sizes within a sector. In the south-eastern sector, which was allocated to the traders and Kshatriyas, the frequency is much less, while in the western sectors where the artisans and craftsmen inhabited, the individual plot sizes are smaller and the frequency of the sub-sector roads is greater.

Jan 16/87

Extreme consideration is observed to have been given to the major roads and their intersections in the planning of the town. The city has played a dominant role as a major trading centre for the region. The commercial uses along the major roads, Rajmarg, as well as the treatment of intersections which become large gathering spaces have contributed significantly to the imageability and growth of the city.

Public Places
Given the period of its founding, it is not surprising that the city would lack the amenities which are commonly accepted today. Being a monarchy the palace precinct became the hub of major public activities. This precinct, suitably, occupies two of the city sectors and has large squares and appropriate structures to deal with the various administrative functions. The most distinguishing feature in the entire urban fabric of Old Jaipur is the *chaupar,* which occurs at the intersections of the east-west road by the three north-south roads. Creating an open square, thrice the width of the major roads at the inter sections, the city gained three such squares measuring about 100 by 100m. Considering that the city was planned for about 60,000 persons, these squares could definitely be considered adequate enough for public gatherings on festive occasions. It is necessary to recall that motorised movement did not exist during the period, and until 40 years ago, must have formed a unique urban experience, enhanced by the controlled facade treatment enveloping it.

Besides these three chaupars, large and small pickets of open spaces occur within each of the sector's constituent mohallas. These usually served groups of houses that clustered around them. It has been observed that when such open spaces in the residential mohallas occur within easy access from the major roads, they are being used for commercial activities.

The location and treatment of temples received special attention in the old city. At all the gates in the fort walls, as well as the chaupars, large temples were located. Records indicate that temples which already existed on the site when the town was laid out, were incorporated within the plan. Thus, one may find a few temples right in the middle of major roads.

The temples on the major roads are the only structures allowed to break the otherwise uniform facades along these roads. This was done by allowing a single flight of steps leading from the roads to the main floor of the temples, which invariably occurs at a much higher level. Such an architectural consideration makes the temples stand out as distinguished landmarks in the entire urban character of Old Jaipur.

It may be worth mentioning here that in the 18th century formal education, as we know of it today, did not exist. Only a small segment of the society had any education and that too on religious scriptures. Thus one finds at Jaipur several large temples having two to three courts in successions (courts measuring as large as 25 by 25m), surrounded by wings deep enough to accommodate teaching areas. Indeed, these structures are presently used for formal schooling. The courts are observed to be used as outdoor classrooms as well as for games like basketball, badminton and such.

As discussed earlier, the facades along the major roads throughout the city were designed and constructed by the state to ensure aesthetic control. Thus one finds a continuous shopping arcade along the road with residential structures rising behind it. Yet anther method of facade control employed was in maintaining a uniformity in colour. The major roads were abutted by building facades with pinkish stone (later terracotta wash was used), a phenomenon that earned Old Jaipur its name of the 'Pink City'.

Response to Climate and Resource

The design of the old city of Jaipur responds very well to the hot climate. The close-knit urban structure reduces the surface area of the built form in relation to its volume. The radiation absorbed from the sun therefore decreases significantly. The houses are attached to each other in groups in order to maximise the common walls which are not exposed to elements. Even the spaces between the buildings within the sectors are narrow so as to exclude the sun. The external shaded spaces can thus become the extensions of the built form which the public can use. The climatic constraints thus create intimate external spaces which also relate well to the human scale. At the urban level, the spaces between the built form as well as the open spaces within buildings give a sieve-like structure to the overall fabric. Thus, whilst individual dwellings may not be well cross-ventilated, the urban mass as a whole becomes porous for cooling at nights due to a large surface area radiating the heat absorbed. In any case, the proportions of the courts ensure that during the day, direct radiation on the horizontal surface is minimised by shadows.

A typical Old Jaipur house sited within the close-knit town fabric is observed to be in complete harmony with the hot-dry climatic conditions of the region. The plan organisation is basically introverted, around a court, and the treatment of facades and openings indicates a sensitive response to climate. This introverted character suited very well the lifestyle of the people of that period.

At the dwelling level, one sees all the features which one would expect to see in a hot climate. The walls are thick and have a high thermal resistance. Minimum openings are provided in the external walls to prevent the hot summer winds from entering the house. Larger windows with wooden shutters could have helped exclude the hot summer winds with the added advantage of permitting cross ventilation when opened at nights. However, the scarcity of timber must have ruled out this nights option. The method used for cooling the houses is a passive circulation of air rather than direct ventilation. Invariably, the small windows are further protected by overhangs known as *chhajas*. Indeed, on the east-west streets even small chhajas can protect most of the external wall surfaces from direct solar radiation. The roofs, which receive considerable solar radiation, are heavily insulated by the layers of *surkhi* embedded with stone chips which overlay the stone roofing planks.

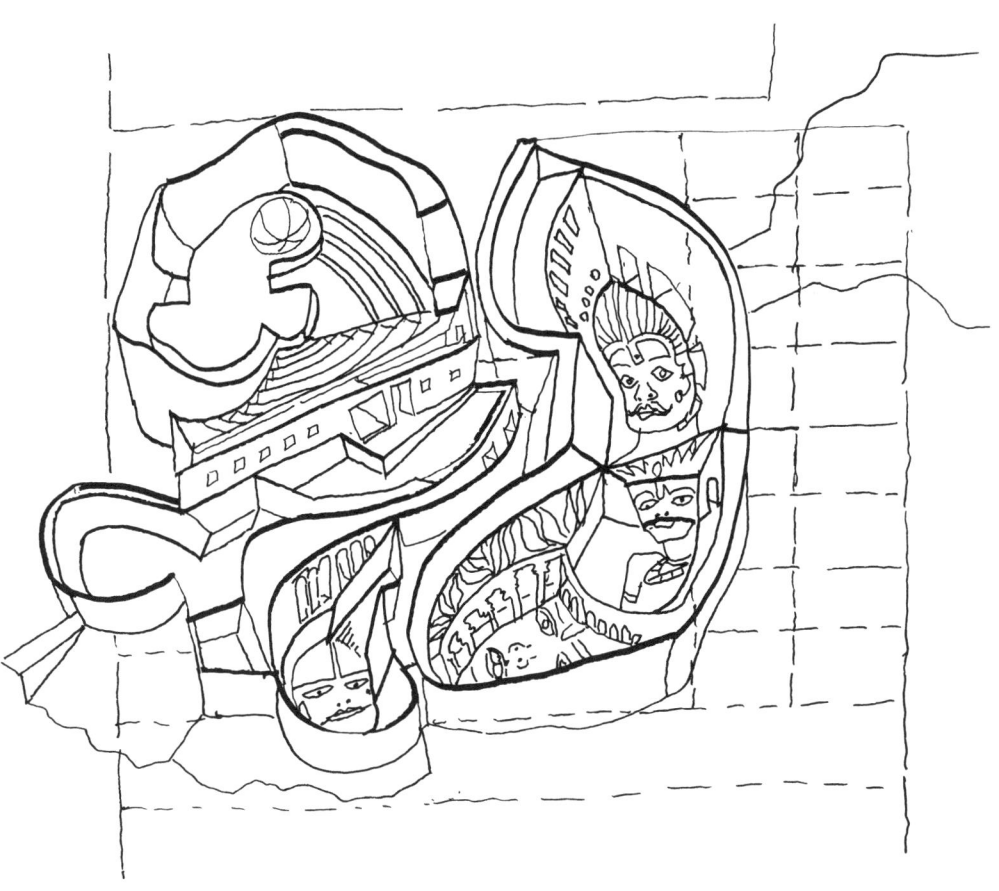

To achieve passive cooling, courts are provided in all the houses. The courts work by trapping cool layers of air at night. This trapped air is prevented from heating during the daytime by limiting the courts' plan dimensions in relations to their height. It is observed that in larger houses, rather than providing an equally large court, a series of smaller courts is provided.

Residential Character
Mohallas
As discussed earlier, the typical Old Jaipur sector size of 800 by 800m is ideally suited to predominantly pedestrian modes. In absolute terms, this makes the inhabitant at the centre of the sector only 300m. away from the commercial activities along the major roads, which is about five minutes of walking distance.

Individual *mohallas* within the grid of sub-sector roads are found to be varying between 160 by 160m to 110 by 110m in size in different sectors inhabited by people of different ranks, and varying residential plot sizes. Observations have indicated that such mohallas typically accommodate about 40 to 50 residential plots. This number is highly conducive in making the mohalla a cohesive social and cultural subgroup. Since the inhabitants of mohallas invariably belong to a single subcaste and pursue the same trades, the social cohesion becomes stronger.

This implies that apart from sharing common facilities like a drinking water well, workshop areas etc, their religious practices and festivals including the presiding deity in the mohallas temple would be similar. All such factors contribute to strengthening their community ties.

Observations
The studies carried out by the team at various scales from sector to individual house plan of the old city of Jaipur generated a number of observations which were felt to be a part of the principles that must have been adopted from the Vastu Shastra in the planning of the city. These observations can be described

under four major heads which broadly reflect the aims that were intended to be achieved through the city's planning.

Environmental Concern

The planning of the old city reflects an excellent response to the hot-dry climate of the region, which is prone to dust storms in summer. The close-knit fabric of the city and the introverted character of the built environment help to keep out the harsh climate. The orientation of major and minor roads are such that according to the context, the streets get varying amounts of shade. By locating the major axial road, running east-west along the ridge, the city's layout takes advantage of the natural topography for drainage. It is a well-known fact that the old city was the only area that was not affected during the 1981 floods in Jaipur. Since water and vegetation were scarce, wells and tanks were treated with importance and trees were planted at such locations that they also served as social meeting places. Rainwater was collected in tanks and was used throughout the year. At the dwelling level, the use of court, shading devices and minimum exposure of the walls to direct radiation helped to achieve thermal comfort.

Efficiency

Efficiency is interpreted as the use of all available resources for the ease and convenience in the activities of the government, business and individuals. Unlike several planned cities and capitals in India, the decision taken by Jai Singh to invite different social groups representing various trades and crafts proved to be beneficial, since it provided the city with an economic base and ensured its survival and growth. Treating all the communities with equal importance helped in promoting efficient interaction in terms of business, trade and communal harmony. Trade was particularly given an impetus by the state which executed the major bazaars and institutions.

The special treatment accorded to temples is noteworthy. Temples did not only enshrine a deity but also served as institutions of learning and generated a sense of community in sociocultural terms.

In terms of the city plan, the average size of a sector, measuring 800 by 800m, is found to be highly suitable to facilitate pedestrian dominated movement. Given this size, the maximum distance a person would walk to reach any major commercial or transport mode would be about 400 to 500m which is approximately a five-minute walk. This not only enhances safety but also attributes a human scale to the city. At the cluster and residential level, the organisation of community spaces and street access are planned so as to promote social interaction and also increase the level of privacy for its residents. The building materials used are those which were available locally and utilised the skills of the local craftsman, thus promoting their trade and expertise.

Flexibility
A remarkable feature of the basic gridiron structure adopted from the Prastara plan in Jaipur is that it allows growth and change on a gradual basis. It is open-ended but not endless. Shifting the north-western falling in the hilly site to the south-eastern corner (Topkhana Hazuri Chaukri) is itself demonstrative of this potential of a gridiron. Also, in a contemporary sense, the plan is extremely democratic in character. The city structure, due to its orthogonal geometry, does not stress a particular spot or activity area. Within the grid, however, despite a similar pattern, the clustering of houses and street network respond to the needs of the people and are not rigidly fixed.

Imageability
The low-key character of the entire urban experience is regarded as a significant aspect of Old Jaipur. Moving along the major road network, and at the chaupars, one is not confronted by imposing edifices like the administrative offices, palaces, memorials and such structures. Despite being founded by a king, there is no expression of his authority or imposition on the lives of the people, which reflects highly on his sensitivity and humane attitude. This character is highlighted by the fact that the axial roads do not terminate at any major public edifices. Visually the openness of the plan is strengthened by long perspectives along the roads which offer views of the temples in the distant hills.

LEARNING FROM OLD JAIPUR

The visual harmony and urban character along axial roads was achieved by executing the bazaars and abutting structures and applying facade controls. The vivid images created of the old city are a result of all these factors intermingling with the rich culture and lifestyle of the people to create a strong identity and character to which the residents and visitors relate and respond strongly.

Urbanism – Old Jaipur

One of the most significant aspects of Old Jaipur's conception and execution is that no effort has been spared to realise both the abstract as well as physical objectives that Jai Singh and Vidyadhar Bhattacharya shared as a vision. This thoroughness is amply evident in Old Jaipur where, whether one is moving along the major roads or within the residential areas, the total urban environment exhibits a well thought out and cohesive character.

BETWEEN NOTION AND REALITY

1989

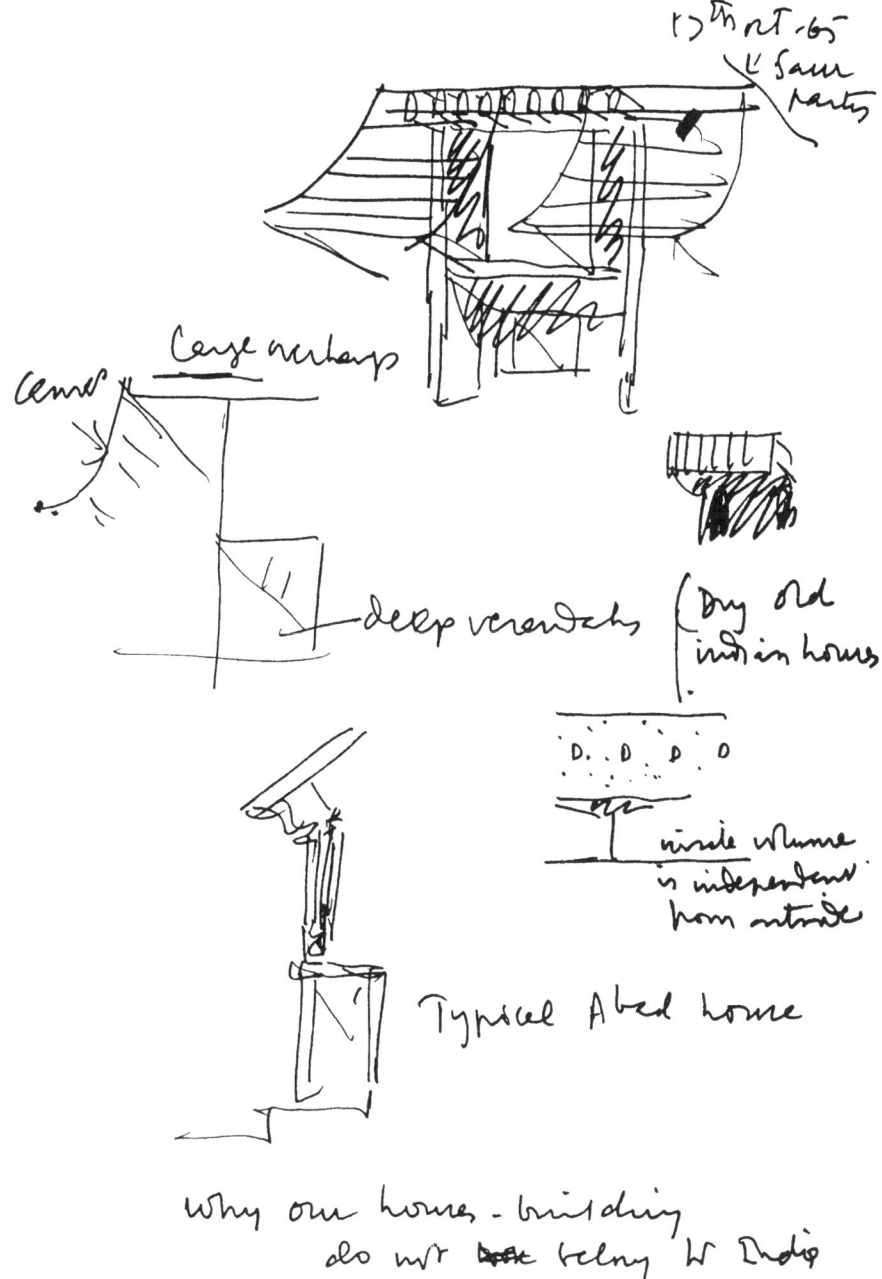

Why our houses - building
do not belong to India
why they could be considered as
from anywhere

Oct 65

Talking about architecture is always a difficult proposition. Architecture is an extremely complex phenomenon, neither purely physical, purely intellectual, nor purely psychic but a comprehensive manifestation of the three and capable of influencing the lives of individuals and communities. It is not often that in an architectural creation the physical, intellectual, and psychic aspects all are understood, translated into a design concept, and carried through in the built form. When that does happen, though, the result rises above the mundane level to be sanctified and revered by generations.

Treating physical needs alone in a built form produces an experience that is body-oriented and a response that is direct. The built form itself is characterised by its emphasis on textural modulations, voluptuous forms, and silhouettes, attributes one finds in folk art. Satisfying only rational demands generates a measure-oriented experience and responses connected to answering specific functional requirements. Many of the socioeconomic considerations in architectural design are interpreted in measurable terms. Architecturally speaking, the approach is toward efficient planning, but designs that are based on mere logic tend to be sterile.

Both of these aspects of architectural design do serve basic needs of the community and the individual. Although emphasis on just one eventually will necessitate changes in the built form as gradually the awareness of the others is felt, together they can lead to a cohesive response. However, the built forms that reflect only the physical and the rational do not necessarily form a sense of unity with the community, and without this they do not become worthy of an emerging heritage. The present reaction against contemporary architecture, with its intellectual and function-oriented styles, clearly indicates its failure in this important respect. Architecture calls for an attempt to address the fundamental need of human beings to be in central relation with themselves and to be in subtle touch with the built form.

In my opinion, supreme among architectural experiences are those which occur along routes of movement and in spaces that could be characterised as pause or ambiguous plural spaces. These spaces activate the human psyche and induce it to sink toward the centre, the mythical world of humans' primordial being. Time and space become internalised, and a deeply-rooted personal identity with the built form gets established. Several of these space-psyche experiences over a period of time generate a set of *spandana* (vibrations), so that the qualitative aspect of the experiences becomes memorable, cherished by the community at large as well as by individual members and passed on to subsequent generations as part of their heritage. Here rituals play a significant role in elevating the psychic response to a built form. Rituals invite considerations of environment, of society, and of humankind, and they endure longer than individuals, society, or even the environment. So when space is a place for observance of rituals or is associated with rituals, it becomes sacred. At this point, I think architecture emerges. The built form becomes timeless and has a quality that goes beyond the obvious; a meaning and profoundness that transcend the particular person or action. It enriches the entire living order.

Hindu temples are classic examples of architecture that fulfils these purposes. An elaborate sequencing of spaces starts with the open space at the entrance and culminates at the *garbhagrha,* the 'sanctum sanctorum', a dark and totally enclosed area except for the doorway through the *nrtyamandapa,* the dance pavilion, open on its other three sides. Of different sizes and with varied ceiling heights as well as degrees of enclosure, the spaces are in tune with the nature of the rituals assigned to each one of them – from the more festive in character at the entrance to the meditative in the garbhagrha.

Most of us, irrespective of personal beliefs, are moved when we pay a visit to a temple. And I have been trying to understand this 'moving' experience in architectural terms with the objective that it could be applied to create new built forms of lasting value. It seems to me that the pauses, transitional spaces, and thresholds act as catalytic agents for the built forms and the individual or the community to enter into a dialogue at their level of comprehension – a dialogue that gives direction to the community at large in the realisation of goals for the self and society.

As a result of the holistic experience they generate, they finally become institutions. And it is within the framework of the values that these institutions then establish that and the individual's freedom of expression is encouraged. In the effort to emulate the spiritual experience of being in constant contact with the centre and the periphery, each individual strives for excellence.

No insignificant part of our architectural heritage was achieved in this special way. For example, it is said that during the execution of the rock-cut temple complex at Ellora, the master architect would come to the site only once every few years, to set broad guidelines, and left much of the detail to the individuals working there. The exercise of creative freedom by each architect-sculptor within an overall framework, across the centuries, produced an extremely rich architectural experience. Long corridors flanked by myriad sculptured columns, varied ceiling heights, courtyards, and especially sensitive modulation of light and rhythm have for all these years allowed visitors to Ellora a pause to regain personal faith and identity.

Similar concepts to enhance the psychic experience were adopted in the larger urban fabric, through the organisation of a hierarchical network of interior and open spaces, large and small, public and domestic, that serve to bring people together. Buildings associated with rituals, such as shrines, became the active centres of the community – routes leading to them became sanctified places of cultural and ritual performances – and evolved into temple cities like Srirangam. At the domestic level, porches and balconies became the outward physical expression of the family and its contact with the community, and the open court (atrium) within the dwelling acted as the communication centre for the family. The court in a house and the central open space in an urban structure are, according to traditional Indian tenets of planning, presided over by Lord Brahma. Being open to the sky, these spaces infuse in individuals and the community the consciousness of nature, as well as bringing the occupants into daily contact with the supernatural and the mythical, and giving them a sense of humility.

The realisation that the psychic experiences in architecture are central and that physical and intellectual experiences are to be developed around them is what fascinates me. It has led me to a critical viewing of the traditional architecture of my environment where a holistic experience is strongly felt, as well as to an effort to identify the spatial characteristics and architectural tools that made it possible, in order to recreate such an experience in my work. The urge to design a built form rooted in all its aspects to the land where it stands has preoccupied my thinking for several years. Below I describe a few of the institutional projects in which I have attempted to incorporate the elements of pause and ambiguity and emphasise the kinds of routes of movement I observed and studied. If nothing else, it certainly is such spatial characteristics that set projects apart from much contemporary design practice, including my own of a few years ago.

Indian Institute of Management, Bangalore

Emperor Akbar established his well-known capital Fatehpur Sikri in the 16th century. Although it remained unoccupied except for a few years, it is appreciated universally for its scale, clarity, architectural style and, most significant of all, its spatial organisation. Here one discovers solutions to the now familiar problem of how to extend or add buildings and yet relate them, how to ensure that all the individual, constituent parts of the complex evoke the sense of belonging to a larger fabric. And it is not surprising that the tools employed at Fatehpur Sikri, to simultaneously functionally divide and unite the various buildings in a complex, are the same as those used in planning temples in South India.

The response is achieved by adopting a system of major corridors for movement along which activity areas are disposed. The corridors themselves are very much like an umbilical cord in an extended family, separating the individual members and yet connecting them, even though tenuously. And within the network of corridors, the space between the activity areas become courts having the sanctity of Brahman, into which the activities can extend and related ones take place.

urban design
Bldg- with
public connection

P. Hall   Bhadra ⑫ urban design

growth/flexibility Garden Campus / Pergola Shade
⑧ Campus - Courty'ard & Trees
13
14   11 m⑧ garden - Courts outdoor teaching
15 (1978) inter connectivity
        extensibility units

Vault ⑨ Basement ⑥ Form/ Frameless
walls Sangath ⑰
Plinth (1980) Passive Energy System

Hut/ ground plinth
experience   City Plan   Bldg Face Facade

⑩ Vidyadharnagar ⑱
     ⑧⑤   Energy Conscious City
       ⑪   clusters, neigh borhood
            clean city, employment
            choice

     Aranya ⑰⑥ LIC housing.

     ⑧⑦   ⑧⑥ ⑧⑦
              ⑧A Delhi
                   extensions House
                   Massing

double structure | earth bound
plinth / ompuri ⑲ Skybound

Ephemeral

(12) Crystalline Architecture
reflections — Transparencies

(BDB) HighTech urban / shape / orientation urban terms
small town (350m)
30 lakh sft   Ephemeral   Mythic

(13)   china mosaic mf (1994)
                                         cmfa
                                         plinth/mf

                        underground
                        Architectural Issues

Bldg/above grn
Bldg/below grn   Form/Formlessness

green — is it a garden a Hag Tejal house (3B)
                              Form as multiple layers
                              3 distinctly separate
                              at each floor level
                              light   perforated
                              overhangs, verandahs mf
  garden   china Mosaic mf
  directional

              (912)
(14) Sawai Gandharva
  = Layers of staircases — walls/rooms

These courts regenerate the primordial sense of continuity, growth, and tenuous linkages of the living and their habitat environment.

Also of great interest to me at Fatehpur Sikri is that the presence of the buildings is felt very strongly, in spite of their being relatively small. This is made possible by the well-conceived relation of the building to the ground and sky, and the backdrop of the linking corridor.

With an extensive academic programme that stretches and changes over the years, the institute similarly required a design that would attend to continuity and growth and give the buildings an individual and common identity. Bangalore's climate is comfortable, and the city is full of lush green lawns and trees. Incorporating the characteristics of the local environment into the design, the 'building' in this project includes the outside spaces, where academic exchange also can take place. Functional and physical attributes of the design were attuned to the local traditions of pavilion-like spaces, courtyards, and ample provision for grass and plants.

Because these local elements by themselves do not necessarily touch everyone, the design also included long and unusually high (three-storey) corridors with innumerable vistas of focal points generating a dialogue with one's self. These corridors are sometimes seen open, through the use of pergolas and skylights. To further heighten the spatial experience, the width of the corridors was modulated in many places to allow casual sitting and interaction. Access to classrooms and administrative offices was provided through these links as well as to generate constant activity. Owing to the varying rhythm of the solids and voids, ie wall and opening, coupled with direct or indirect natural light, these links change in character during the different times of the day and seasons offering the students and the faculty occasion to feel the presence of nature even while they are inside. The structure and enriching the activities pursued within the building because they become one with the larger, total world. Architecturally, the links appear and disappear, and this gives a sense of being and not being wherein the actual becomes notional. In the mornings and evenings, the sun's golden rays are reflected in the glazed windows, and the long corridors with the main central court surrounded by classroom walls give a feeling of being in a place not unknown to one's inner being.

Sangath, Ahmedabad

This programme envisioned a complex that would encourage activities in the areas of fine and technological arts related to architecture, planning and crafts. Spaces were needed for long- and short-term workshops and seminars, and to accommodate a professional architectural firm and an office for the Vastushilpa Foundation – in other words, for many functions.

In the initial stages of planning, a flow pattern of activities and their volumetric space requirements were determined; this generated not only the spatial but also the structural dimensions of the complex. Conditions in the hot, dry climate of Ahmedabad and various energy-efficient designs, primarily based on passive response, were evaluated for the control of interior heat. The sum total of these rational needs was then studied volumetrically, and the building-site relationship was established. Since, at a sensuous level, it was felt essential that form, light and space should be integrated, a design combining these with functional, climatic and technological considerations was evolved. Somehow, though, the model still did not express the vitality of the activities planned for the complex; it seemed capable of allowing only the measurable functions.

In order for the built form to match the dynamic concept of Sangath (in the vernacular it stands for moving together to a goal), it appeared that equally dynamic articulating methods had to be discovered to give another dimension to the transitional spaces and to continuously generate experiences of the ambiguous. One way of doing this was to incorporate into the built form a series of contrasts, such as spaces that push below ground and surge above ground, or high spaces, flooded with light, and low spaces, dimly lit.

The entire building has three different, closely interlinked structural systems. One comprises load-bearing brick walls carrying the vaulted roof; the second, with a retaining wall and brick column structure of irregular shape, supports a flat roof; the third employs load-bearing walls combined with post-and-beam structure to carry heavier loads. Each system has been optimally used to create the variety of spaces described earlier. Likewise, three means of allowing light into the interior were devised: one through normal windows punctured in the wall, another through a skylight, the third through direct penetration from the flat roof through the glass brick. Such spaces, articulated by particular structural systems, make the built form specific.

However, all these methods of articulation remained technical, only marginally moving beyond the physical, falling short of touching the psyche. At this juncture efforts turned to building the surprises in a certain rhythm, or sequence. If a building stretches, is cut into many parts, is seen as fragments, direct confrontation with it is replaced by a sense of gradual transformation that diverts the mind. The long double structures and unexpected unassigned spaces heighten and accentuate the experience of surprise.

Finally, to bring the individual into focus, it was decided to underplay the overall scale of the built form. This has been accomplished through a practice that, although widely used in traditional temple architecture, is rather unusual in the contemporary context, relating to the treatment of the plinth (base). The articulation of the interior spaces as described earlier led to sinking certain areas and elevating others. Articulating the plinth in several ways, one notices as one approaches the building, has mitigated the external massing of the building. The approach walkway gradually becomes steps for gathering and, through a series of platforms, culminates at the terrace where the upper level entrance is situated. This low base and the high roof vaults may evoke in an Indian mind the proportions of the deity's face and the tall *shikhara* (crown) of a temple with its low base. The sunken floor level at the lower entrance summons the experience of entering the ancient caves. The roundly-articulated edges of the vaults and other surfaces accessible from the low terraces generate a firm relationship with the ground, like that found in a Buddhist *stupa*.

The ambiguous, open-ended character of the built form starts to reveal itself right at the entrance, which makes one wonder about where to move and how to reach the sanctum. In achieving a destination, there are many ways to go. You can find your own space, in your own time, through your own movement. And the space has to be something beyond just a structure; it has to be like a book, to reach different people and give them the kind of information they need at certain points of time and space. Sangath has two entrances, one at six feet above and the other at three feet below ground level. Both finally reach the same place but through different paths.

Many visitors, learned or otherwise, architects and laypeople, have felt an unusual experience at Sangath. Since one is touched at some centre of one's being, I feel that I have succeeded in activating the psychic aspect of the relationship between architecture and the community.

Gandhi Labour Institute, Ahmedabad

I have observed over the years that architecture in a hot, dry climate has evolved a dual system of structuring: there is one main system to support the activity areas and another to support an envelope that protects the inside from the harsh weather conditions. This building within a building with a central court corresponds to the body and the soul, with the house representing the body and the open court its soul, symbolising Brahman. Most often this court evidences a formal geometric character, whereas the external edge of the building responds to the configuration of the site.

A second characteristic I have observed and incorporated into this design, as well as that of Sangath, is the way sacred buildings relate to the ground and articulate the plinth. Raising a plinth makes a building seem no longer ordinary but important. Access with reverence is also made possible by breaking surfaces to avoid solidity; the silhouette thus achieved establishes a strong relation with the earth and the sky.

The qualities of the village square also provided inspiration for this design. Usually featuring a large tree under which a platform is raised, the square is essentially a court surrounded by buildings, but the scale and modulation of the buildings somehow efface social disparities, create a cohesive community, and give the place a sense of belonging. These three varied aspects of an accessible yet respectful place, within a small-scale urban setting and responding to the local climate, constitute the main theme of the Gandhi Labour Institute.

This state-owned institute, which conducts research, training, seminars, and workshops in labour management and welfare, is relatively small but has the potential to grow. The functional demands are similar to those of any such institute: a library, classrooms, seminar rooms, administration, trainees' accommodations, a canteen. In order to generate a design comprehending the functional, symbolic, and notional levels, I referred to and adopted the models of an inner court of a large *haveli* in Jaisalmer and a temple at Vadtal, as well as a typical village square, and I employed a series of thresholds and linkages of varied scales to accentuate the meaning of these images.

The Gandhi Labour Institute's front plaza with a long, wide flight of approaching steps allows sufficient time for the visitor to absorb the experience of this otherwise imposing building. The long linkages, with their high exhibition space and narrow movement areas between the internal and external courtyards, connect all the functional areas of the complex, through visual or actual contacts. In the central inner court, with its linkage to the outer court, amphitheatre, dining area, and the terraces of the dormitories, one has the feeling of being in a village square, as an individual or as a member of the community and its small pool captures for the observer sun, moon, and sky reflected in it.

The counterbalancing of different structural systems, along with constantly changing floor configurations and the skewing of the dormitory block from the right-angle geometry of the institute's building, are natural reflexes much like our constant inhaling and exhaling. It is through all these elements that an attempt is made to relate an individual's centre to the physical and intellectual world.

Architecture is not a temporary affair. If we can make space that can exalt itself, it will take root, have meaning and last a long time.

GROWTH, CHANGE AND DEVELOPMENT IN URBAN CENTRES

1996

Change is the basis of any life form, any creation, according to Hindu philosophy. Creation, destruction and recreation being an unending chain of happenings, the 'form' is an ever-changing phenomenon. What remains is the 'energy' balance. Even life is a transient phase between the past and the future, between birth and reincarnation, each of the phases prepare one for the next. As in the metamorphosis of a frog or the butterfly, the ultimate goal/direction is set but phases and forms to reach the same are distinct. Thus change is synonymous to evolution in Hindu way of life as it becomes ingrained and no longer remains alien.

This led to tolerance, diversity and flexibility. Which is why even the extremes can coexist in India. As counterpoints they become mutual references and an integral part of a self-balancing system ensuring the continuum and endurance. The reason it can do so is because in the Indian psyche, notions remain critical rather than realities. This is true for space as well. This is best exemplified by the ritualistic creation of a sacred space for a Hindu marriage. Here four banana leaves at the corners of a temporary pavilion can become the enclosure for sanctifying a marriage.

It is imperative for any architecture to inspire the psyche, touch notions and pamper the aspirations of the people. Architecture thus becomes an exercise in place making (not a space making) – an environmental setting for invoking *prana*, the breath of life, a desired participation from the user. A true dialogue between the place and the people. Architecture of cities is all about the mutual communications – a symbiosis.

When this happens, urban centres take different forms and accommodate an entirely varied spectrum of activities throughout the daily cycle on a continuing basis which is full of life and vitality. On the other hand seemingly comfortable spaces of the modern city with so-called generous space standards remain empty and unused for not feeling the pulse of the place and people.

What then is the pulse of Indian spaces?

A non-linear conception of time, predominance of notion over reality, balance between individual identity and collective conformity and flexibile interpretation for coexistence of paradoxes are the key elements of the Indian psyche.

Time in India is a helical and not a linear phenomenon. Destinations can be reached by all without the standardisation or predictability of time, scale or movement. This lets each one of the members of the civic community explore, and thereby evolve, at one's own pace and by personal preferences. This is an attribute which ensures interaction.

Equally potent tools are the myths and symbols. Conjuring associations and inspiring notions, it makes an object come alive to dialogue on a one-to-one basis. Interpretation can be as many but the basic communication is the same.

This aspect of conformity within identity, ie collective conformity with individual identity, marks yet another attribute of vitality in India. Each particle like an atom is an entity – an order – a system complete on its own, yet there is a common bond of values, allegiance to another order of systems (values) and thus conforming mutually and overall. What we call heterogeneous homogeneity or the unity in diversity.

This aspect of atom and universe, microcosm and cosmos refers to the schema of centre and sub-centre. Individual aspirations and societal norms create tenuous yet rich relationships between the various parts of the ensemble. The richness of the concept lies in its freedom to evolve from whole to part or parts forming a whole. Apparent paradoxes can be combined, as intention rather than actions get highlighted.

Architecturally speaking, experience rather than expressions is essential. Traditional Indian architecture has demonstrated such an approach and it has always stood the test of time.

Changes continue to take place even now. Perhaps more rapidly in the recent past than ever. Change per se may not be a new phenomena for the city but its pace and manner may be. Isolated buildings become islands within their own compounds, and oblivious to their surroundings, they portray an utter sense of indifference to its place and people, paving the way for pampering the egos of a few.

Social structure and collective values have been held at ransom. No wonder no civic space or institution has been created for people to relate to – to identify with. The city has transferred, but not in the fuller sense, transformed, as mutations have somewhere lost the track of the basic pulse of place. Values in flux are apparent in the chaos in social as well as physical order. An intervention is called for. Mutation is needed for three fundamental reasons. One, to resolve the basic process of evolution as the city organism has perhaps reached its threshold. Second, to regain the balance by undoing, reconditioning what has been done in a past decade and third, to set a new direction for its growth with a newer set of values, demands and aspirations.

The architecture of interface has to be reinvented. The architecture of thresholds has to be reinterpreted. The architecture of the unbuilt has to be recalled and architecture as place-making and a behavioural setting has to be rediscovered from the basic flexible mould of the city that has always transformed and metamorphosed without a sense of mutation. This is what I call the pulse of Indian city. The magic!

Habitat in the Indian context implies a range of situations typical to a developing society with scarce resources and rich and diverse traditional heritage. The major urban centres present a dismal picture with rapid proliferation of squatter and slum settlements, over-congested streets, inadequate public transport systems, growing unemployment, lack of access to basic services like drinking water and sanitation, inappropriate urban management and growing civic disturbances. The net result is a continual decline of the quality of life in urban centres today. A vast majority of the population can barely meet its daily needs. Even those few

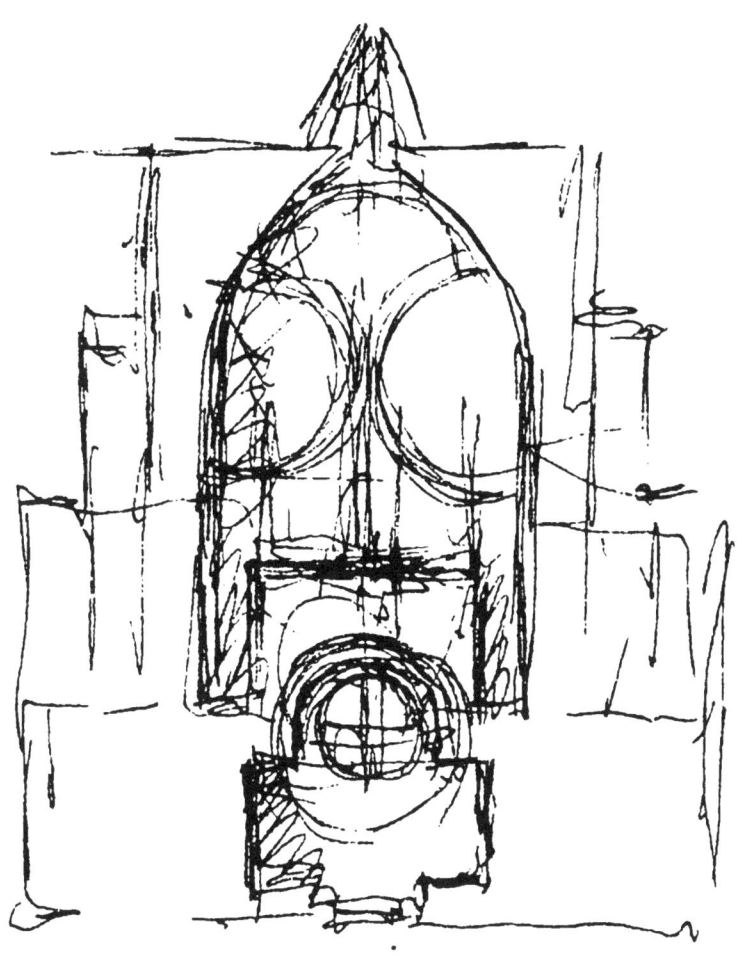

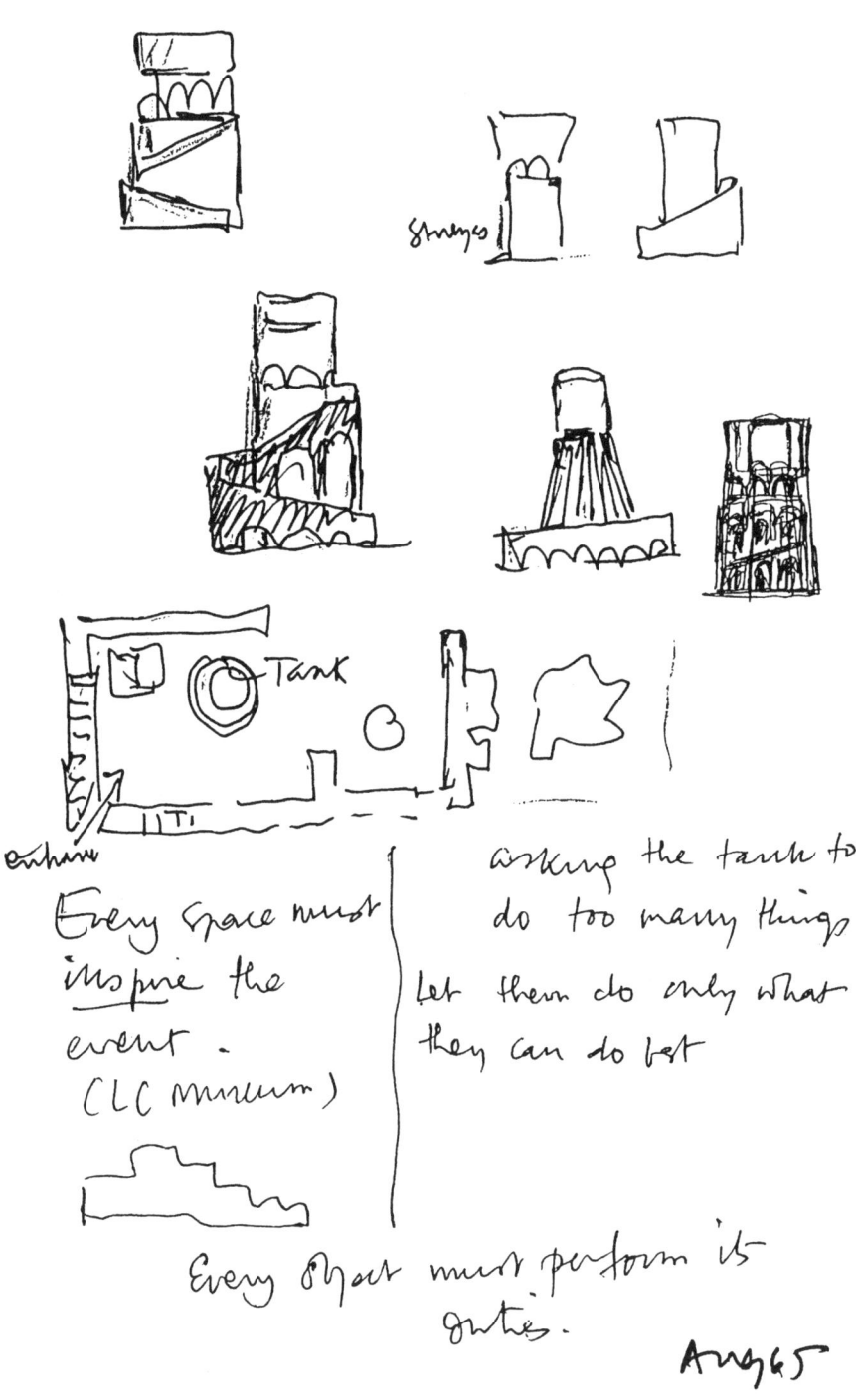

Every space must inspire the event.
(LLC museum)

asking the tank to do too many things
Let them do only what they can do best

Every object must perform its duties.

Aug 65

who can afford a house of their own have to accept an environment ill suited to their sociocultural aspirations or the way of life.

A problem as complex as this necessitates a chain of pertinent and value-based codes to function as bridges between the ideals and contemporary realities of the society. These codes can act as the channels that transform the body of thought of a profession into the aspired to and cherished vision.

Human settlements, wherever they exist or emerge, are organised systems and places of productive and creative activities. Houses, not implying mere shelters with four walls and a roof, always remain living environments around which the entire realm of the family and community's well-being is created. Clusters of houses when multiplied become communities full of life, diversity and vitality. Hence the role of public agencies in housing is to be increasingly visualised as a facilitator of living environments and not as a producer of house prototypes stacked in efficient rows.

Such a role and supportive policies, to promote a progressive development of shelter by the people themselves, are absolutely necessary if we want the inhabitants to be hopeful for their prosperous future. This attitude will naturally allow consideration of culture, social norms and customs as the major factor in determining the shelter needs. To achieve this there is a need to evolve a new set of codes for human habitats which recognises the sociocultural ethos of the place which stipulates harmony, balance and a sense of life in various quantitative, as well as qualitative, and physical as well as social, facets of human habitat. Our attempts, through research and its applications in real projects, are focused on examining the scope for a rational, objective and culture-specific assessment of the quality of life in a human habitat and ways and means to achieve the same through settlement designs. Aranya and Vidyadhar Nagar are examples in this case.

LE CORBUSIER:
THE INDIAN INCARNATION

1996

Standing today in front of Mme Helene de Roche – Directrice, Fondation de la Suisse and Mons Michel Richard – Director, Foundation Le Corbusier, my colleagues from the Atelier Le Corbusier as well as distinguished scholars and friends, I am enthralled to recount my sojourn with Mons Le Corbusier. My mentor and guru, with whom I spent four very impressionable years at his studio in Paris and subsequently, my association with him at Chandigarh and Ahmedabad.

I remember how my day would begin with a view of the Pavilion Suisse from my third floor window of Maison du Japon. It was my senior colleague Takamasa Yoshizaka who managed to get me a room there and I stayed on for almost three years, with this wonderful view. Paris for me was a strange new world. I came from Pune, a small city, went to neighbouring Bombay for my education and then via London landed in Mons Le Corbusier's studio. Thanks to another colleague from the atelier, German Samper, who after meeting me in Hoddesdon and London during the CIAM Conference, recommended me to Mons Le Corbusier.

I was vegetarian, did not speak a word of French and had not much background of contemporary world architecture. While working at 35 Rue de Sèvres – drawings, spoken voices and body language were my basic tools of communication. Thinking back, I feel these shortcomings actually gave me an advantage. I became most attentive all the time, with all my senses alert to catch the subtlest nuances. Mons Le Corbusier reciprocated this diligence by paying more attention to me and spending more time on my desk. He took me under his wing, became my guru and spent hours on the drafting board, explaining in cryptic language all that he wanted me to understand and draw. It was his gestures, his voice and his drawings in various coloured pencils and pastels that made me learn and feel the life, the environment, the moods and the spaces that he was drawing and simultaneously describing.

While working on the High Court Central Hall sections that he asked me to draw, he arrived, superimposed drawings and created round apertures in the three, freestanding large walls of the entrance hall. He explained how he tried to connect them to the end walls of the central hall as well as to the adjoining ramp located at a right angle. He then explained how a single projecting beam or a parapet height of 140cm could create a different sense of space by drawing a sketch of a standing human figure next to the parapet wall. He then showed me how to connect the main facade of the High Court and its end walls. On them he drew the niches and rounded the edges of the floating parasol and drew shadows suggesting the High Court orientation and its reflection in the water pond below. For me, who had hardly seen a monumental building even in India, such scales and ways of drawing appeared incomprehensible. Often to explain, he would open his sketchbook and tell me the stories about his stay in Chandigarh or his visits to nearby villages. He would show the drawing of a local *charpoy,* Punjabi women with a child, a large mango tree and large-winged birds flying across the vast empty sky. He would say 'Doshi – don't you have such birds flying in your house and making nests in the cap of the ceiling fan? Isn't your way of living with everything around similar?' It would be my turn then to tell him about how I understood our culture, customs, rituals and our family life.

A few months later, Le Corbusier arrived and gave me a sketch on the back of a folder and said, 'My new client Surottam Hutheesing is the president of the Mill Owners' Association. They want to build an office building in Ahmedabad. Have you been there?' I said that I had visited it six years ago. He described the site adjoining the very wide and dry river Sabarmati. There were no trees and the plot faced east and west. He said, 'They have no specific programme, few offices, one conference room and a large hall for 60 to 80 persons for the Association's meetings. Here is a sketch.' It was a stamp-size plan and a sketch of a section showing a ramp leading from the road to the first floor. Three offices on ground and first floor and a double-height second floor with a mention of a conference hall. Without further explanation, he left. Naturally, I asked Maisonnier, the senior architect, how to proceed. He said, 'Look at this sketch carefully. There are two parallel walls shown and major openings on the west and east side. Mons Le Corbusier wants the road and the river to be physically and visually linked.'

This was my first examination. To interpret and formulate a scheme. With the help of Maisonnier, Iannis Xenakis (who treated me like his younger brother) and Samper, I worked out a sketch. I referred to his books, watched the others work on the Sarabhai and Jaoul houses, High Court and the Secretariat schemes. After a week or so, Corbusier came, he watched me, saw the plans and made another sketch. He had created a flowing central space, directly connecting the ramp from the access road to the river pushing all offices towards the sidewalls. A few weeks later, he came again, sat and reworked the scheme at 1:100 scales. This time he restructured the plan, located a lift well, created a sheer wall as enclosure for the elevator and drew columns in between the two thick brick walls. I remember how I struggled for weeks to work out the conference hall on the second floor. Whatever I tried, his only comment was, 'Perhaps you seem to know better.' When he saw my fan-shaped plan of the auditorium and left, I realised something was wrong with my approach. I tried again. After a few days, seeing me lost and dejected, he sat on the stool, placed a yellow tracing paper and started sketching and explaining how people arrive from a staircase or elevator, and how they would enter the hall if they wanted to attend.

He said, 'Some always want to just peek, sit for a chat and then go away.' Then he drew a small window and a hidden side entry. He said, 'Some may stand behind so to create space, some may sit very close to the dais, the speaker's pew. Let's draw a few random chairs at the rear.' In the end he encircled the layout and created the most unusual enclosed space. Thus a free-flowing, curvilinear wall plan emerged – functional and particular. Then he took another paper, said, 'We must find some natural light', and drew the section with the curvilinear floating roof, detached from the main slab. Then came the supporting beams and a terraced garden on the lifted rooftop. As if possessed, he drew another section with a mezzanine floor in a small area of the second floor and an access to the terrace saying, 'Let people get fresh air and a view of the moon light.' Somehow, space for the toilets was not located. He drew circular intertwined bathrooms with a vertically connecting service duct for the pipes. Then he attached them to one side of the wall and said, 'Let them enjoy going around these spaces.'

Decades later, I realised how these spaces, intuitively done, have become experientially rich, free and natural.

I still don't know how he managed to create such an experience. Perhaps he was guided by his inner force to see the world afresh, similar to the casting off of one's skin, to be reborn. In the process, he created a new language, and it was not yet another experiment but the very essence of what he had learned all along. He was constantly observing, searching, interpreting and transforming natural phenomena, objects, plants and whatnot. Anything he saw he adopted and transformed as if for his own pleasure. For example, he talked of the way local inhabitants used their scarce resources. He said, while in India, 'I too follow the custom of using only one bucket full of water and a tumbler for bath, or eat the same way that the food is served, or even study the multiple ways Indians use their clothing fabric.' During one of our trips to the old city of Ahmedabad he saw very small shops stacked one on top of another. Not believing how small the space could be, he stretched himself between the two parallel walls and happily reconfirmed his belief of providing smaller cubicles, narrowest doors, as well as service spaces to accentuate the major open spaces.

I remember how Le Corbusier spoke about the cascading terraces with or without attached balconies or verandahs and how he found them represented in the traditional Indian miniature paintings. He appreciated the existence of such an intimate relationship that Indians have with art and real life. To me, the facades of the Shodhan House with terraces at different levels under the large parasol, or the large lawn and the vegetable garden of the Sarabhai House, or the pavilion-like floors and the roof of the Mill Owners' Association building or his proposal to have hydroponics on the terrace of the Cultural Complex, echo his reinterpretation of our local traditions.

While visiting the construction site of the Ahmedabad Textile Industries Research Association building, he observed and took photographs of the unfinished concrete floor slab surfaces and found a demonstration of the *Béton Brut* in it. Back in

Paris, he asked us to design shuttering patterns with either steel sheets or wooden panels to emphasise not only the surface of the concrete but also its plasticity.

Trips to new places always inspired Le Corbusier with newer thoughts, be it the commonly used furniture or the large horns of the Brahmani bull or its hump. He would not only sketch them but found in them their uniqueness for new expressions in painting, sculpture or architecture. Once, while passing by the cooling towers of the thermal power station of the Ahmedabad Electricity Company he ventured inside, admired the external form and the internal space, tested its acoustic quality and eventually converted it into the chamber for the Chandigarh Assembly building. His inclined slicing of the roof of the cooling tower and adorning it with elements in order to catch the cardinal sun rays on a particular day in a year speaks volumes about his ability to convert highly-developed industrial products into a sacred object of architecture, which incidentally is our tradition. Here one sees how he fused the engineer and the artist in himself. At the micro level he could, likewise, devise new methods to save energy and cost.

I remember him seriously looking at a very famous miniature painting of Radha and Krishna depicting ultimate unity. He was admiring the way both Radha and Krishna were shown holding and playing the flute with one hand each while Krishna was blowing the air and both of them were dancing with one foot intertwined. What fascinated Le Corbusier was their subtle admiration for each other while facing their bodies towards the observer. He copied this painting a few times and finally converted it into his own version. I remember his writing to even Pandit Jawaharlal Nehru about the symbol of the Brahmani bull, the tortoise, the snake, the couch and many others. He had found in them additional meanings, both spiritual and organic. He wanted to use them in his building but avoided this.

Enigma and dynamic balance is what he was constantly searching for. He was much haunted by the enigmatic coolness and romance of the moon's phases, and the twilight zones of dawn and evening when the light would imperceptibly turn into darkness. He knew that it is through constant drawing and writing that the 'muse' would give him insight between the solids-voids, lines and scribbles, to fathom concepts, forms and messages.

His energy and time-conscious attitude is apparent in the way he gave instructions to lay the varying-sized stone flooring. For this he used all the residues and thus created a new rhythmic pattern almost akin to the Indian string instruments.

His vintage *fenêtre undulatoire,* the modulating windows, were born out of this construction solution where choices and circumstantial uncertainties were always present. For him, there was never a typical solution to a typical problem. All were interchangeable and capable of creating new architectural experiences. This act of his is very close to the way classical Indian musicians spontaneously improvise their *ragas* within an overall structure. Perhaps these explorations eventually led him to design the modulated windows used in the Secretariat Building at Chandigarh and at La Tourette.

Curious and open to challenge, he was ever-willing to try. That is why all the buildings by him in Ahmedabad are remarkably different in their spatial experiences and even approach. They are an open book on architecture. They demonstrate many different ways of resolving issues of climate, construction and culture.

The Sarabhai House is a quiet low and meandering recluse amidst nature, a relevant setting for the mother and her two sons. In contrast, Surottam Hutheesing's house was a perfect setting for the flamboyant bachelor. (Hutheesing eventually sold this design to the Shodhans). The house with its overwhelming volumes and cascading terraces under a large and high parasol overlooking the large swimming pool conjures images from the Indian miniature paintings. On the other hand, the Sanskar Kendra, being the place of display, creates neutral backdrops of walls and the introverted spaces become a solid square box in brick with a central court. The Mill Owners' Association building is a fully perforated hollow cube with free standing enclosed masses overlooking the vast Sabarmati River. Let me elaborate this further.

Initially Jean-Louis Véret supervised the four buildings in Ahmedabad and after his departure I took over the finishing. It was only on arrival, I realised what had been materialised. A grand spectacle of volumes, forms, textures, rhythms and infinite variations in light and spatial qualities. It was as if I was visiting the 'open sesame – the hidden treasury of architectural expressions and experiences'. Never had I realised until then what those plans and sections I drew in Paris meant. How easily he had guided me to draw them.

Gradually, I remembered his conversations, sketches and descriptions. It was for me a revelation. True teachings from a guru to a disciple. I realised that it is only in Ahmedabad that Corbusier demonstrated his theories of four typologies of building that he analysed in 1929 when he designed Villa Savoy. This was 1951, a new phase, and especially for Indians. The first of these, explored here at

Ahmedabad, is the residence for Manorama Sarabhai. Villa Sarabhai is a meandering house with the structural rigour of brick vaults but with a flexibility of varied apertures in the load-bearing parallel walls.

It is here that he expresses the power of the vault with deep heavy, crushing beams, which span the large openings and create a spiritual experience of a solid material wall, sliding sideways, like a paper screen.

The interior space of this meandering house simultaneously moves in both directions, constantly revealing its integration with and the presence of the garden, both at ground and roof level and the free-flowing yet contained space with its large pivoted doors. What was for him picturesque then, is now very moving and deeply entrenched to the ground, including on its rooftop. As if it is below ground, there is a semi-dark, dimly-lit hermitage for the lady of the house. Parallel walls parted at irregular distances and supported with oversized heavy beams. A meandering, staggered design. I only understood its real significance when I visited it on my return. Very different from the Jaoul Houses or the Weekend House, this house purposefully denies its own existence. It is indescribable in terms of spaces. It is like a sponge, porous towards the garden. Catalonian vaults of the Jaoul House and the Sarabhai House have totally different impacts through their disposition on the walls, beams and curvature.

On the other hand the museum, the Sanskar Kendra, the Mundaneum that had haunted him since the 1930s, is a perfect example of a cube on stilts, connecting the ground, the sky court and the exhibition space above through a ramp and the free-form reflecting pool. The building floats in spite of its heavy, stuffy columns. While the elevations were drawn and the long creeper trough was added to connect to the terrace level through hydroponics, I remember Mr Ernesto Rogers comparing the proportions of this museum with Leonardo da Vinci's works. Even today, I feel the proportions, scales, size of this building are not matched by the museums he designed in Tokyo and Chandigarh. Again, it was for this project that he sketched and commented, 'very difficult but satisfies the spirit'.

His third sketch which talks of a cube and the free-floating forms within the cube as a very easy, practical and combinable proposal takes a new expression in the Mill Owners' building. Here his box is enveloped with totally opposite types of sun breakers to suit the western and eastern facades and the north and south walls are solid brick walls. But here he intersperses the spaces with free-standing sheer concrete walls and rounded volumes which are light and moving. The structural grid of reinforced concrete columns in this building is broken by the sheer walls, the lift shaft and solid brick end. They not only firmly enclose the box, but also emphasise a directional link between the street and the river. The simple configuration of a ramp leading to the main floor, *piano nobile,* stretches its dominance on the vast but mostly dry riverbed. The double-storey upper floor with its bean-shaped hall and its crescent-shaped room connects this palatial hall to the roof, expressing his message to celebrate life through interconnectedness at all levels. The motif of the crescent-shaped roof garden slab reappears again with greater vigour in the Governor's Palace at Chandigarh which is not yet built.

But the most amazing and the most experiential of the four types is the reincarnation of Villa Savoy turned upside down. That is the Villa Shodhan, originally the Villa Hutheesing. Here, the thin rectangular columns holding the parasol appear to reverse his theory of a city housed on pilotis. Here the parasol creates terraces, shaded areas for meetings and for spending the greater part of night and day, as is depicted in the Indian miniatures.

After the Mill Owners' building design, I was entrusted with the Villa Shodhan project with two alternatives. Le Corbusier's original sketch as published and the other prepared by Emilio Duhart, a Chilean architect who worked for a short while. It was then, that by chance, I had come across traditional Japanese farm houses in a magazine. I was quite amazed to see the way tall and relatively slender wooden columns, square or rectilinear, were braced with rafters of the same size. I observed that these columns could flexibly attach to either the walls or be totally detached. I wondered if for Villa Shodhan, a rectilinear column would be a better proposition than circular, so I asked Le Corbusier. Le Corbusier not only accepted this idea but forthwith drew the new plans and sections.

What we see on the terrace today is the result of his further exploiting the rectangular columns becoming a box with an opening. A suspended *shamiana*-like roof hanging between the main terrace and the parasol. Corbusier had studied miniatures to understand the subtle nuances of shaded, private terraces and balconies. He noticed how the Indian swing created breeze through one's own movement while swinging. By enlarging the diaphragm wall he created multiple images and views as one swing. He also made all the studio apartments out of the wall and column. Finally, except in one area on the ground and on the terrace, the existence of columns and beams disappeared. In the end, Villa Shodhan can be perceived as the total reversal of the Villa Savoy, where the pilotis on the ground became the parasol.

For him, 'chance' meant opportunity. New issues to a challenge meant a virtue. It is very much like our philosophy of open endlessness or ambiguity. Our forefathers believed in the reality of uncertainty and waited for the hidden virtues to come to the surface. That is why all the buildings by him in Ahmedabad are remarkably different in their spatial experiences and even approach. They are an open book on architecture. They demonstrate many different ways of resolving the issues of climate, construction and culture. These four examples are not merely projects. It was a laboratory of ideas. A demonstration of his theories. A dream come true. These four examples are his theories of the thirties, reinvented. The ideas of the growing spiralling museum, the remake of the Esprit Nouveau Pavilion, roof gardens and so on.

Perhaps it was here in India, that he saw greater value in counterpoints or apparent paradoxes. Spiritual meanings, the deeper essence of life, is what he saw in India. The recordings in his diary and letters to his wife give some indication of his confrontation with an ancient, culturally-rich but economically-still developing land. His ultimate statement of interconnectedness and openness, sharing and giving, is at Chandigarh, through the open hand; and his reaffirmed belief in the cosmic connections and to have a pact with nature and technology are aptly expressed in his last testament through the majestic, main enamelled door at the Assembly entrance. However, all these spatial experiences are true *promenade architecturale.* These are perceptions of a variety of spaces, of multiple sensibilities for contemporary life and activities. Perhaps for this reason, he admired most profoundly the quality of activities around the huge water tank, enclosed by the spaces and forms, of the Sarkhej Mosque and Tomb Complex, built in the 17th century. His only comment to me was, 'Doshi, you do not need to go to Acropolis, you have all that we seek from architecture here.'

As anticipated, Le Corbusier's projects in Ahmedabad had an all-India impact because these became a centre of attraction and gave rise to a new centre for contemporary architecture. For the institution builders and the leaders of industry, it signalled revival and resurgence for establishing new institutions.

LE CORBUSIER: THE INDIAN INCARNATION

In the scorching sun one can't walk barefoot, in heat and dust one needs shelter and shade. There is acute scarcity of water in summer and torrential rains and floods during monsoon. Yet life goes on, in rhythmic cycles. In India nothing seems certain except eternal *lila* and the play of the cosmic world.

I am sure, shaken by the Indian kaleidoscopic culture and life, with centuries old customs and the most modern visions, Corbusier must have been challenged. He must have wondered how this country constantly thrived despite droughts, floods, feuds; and yet nurtures great traditions in music, literature, art, food, clothing and architecture. How is it that this country, despite disparities, quarrels and has paradoxes, continues to create such great masterpieces such as the *gopurams* and temples at Madurai, Khajuraho, Akbar's capital city of Fatehpur Sikri, the Taj Mahal and the great architecture of Rajasthan and Kerala. How come Buddhism which was born here disappeared and became a part of Hinduism? How come, despite such diverse regional, climatic and culinary differences, the pilgrimage routes weave the whole country together? Why are the *sadhus, sanyasis* and *yogis*, who have renounced the world, respected by kings, or the men in power?

Against these daily confrontations, his rational European mind must have accepted the situation as is. But somewhere the keen, sensitive mind and intellect must have been affected. He must have smelled the subtle fragrances, the silence that transgresses the solid walls of his previous cultural background.

I have a feeling, that deep within he must have sensed cycles of Indian life with its continuous rituals of birth, marriage and death. In the houses and in the barren lands, he must have sensed the vastness and tightness of spaces, or the nuances of morning or the twilight zone, or the starry, cool nights. The harsh shadows of the afternoon sun with the textures on the walls, created by the details of the traditional buildings, must have given him a sense of what architecture could be.

It is through this door, the symbols on the Assembly roof and the reinterpreted theories on architecture in Ahmedabad, that make us Indians feel close to

Le Corbusier, as if he is the reincarnated version of the earlier *Sthapatis* who created the rock cut temples and caves at Ajanta and Ellora.

Before I conclude, I would like to quote two short instances, which sum up what the world thinks of Mons Le Corbusier. It was the same day Le Corbusier was leaving for Paris via New Delhi. Hesitantly, I asked him if I could join him up to Delhi. 'No,' he said, 'no one ever accompanies me, not even my secretary. They don't keep time or waste any on the way. Nor do I trust myself. That's why I keep this notebook.' Shocked, I lowered my head. I don't know what made him say, 'Okay you can come, provided you are at the bus stand at 7am sharp.' I agreed.

On the way to Delhi, we talked about Gandhiji, Chandigarh and a monument to the Mahatma. He thought of a tree, a platform and a reflecting pool, India's ancient tradition where saints preached. After a while, we reached Delhi. Suddenly, realising that it was 1pm and time for lunch, he asked, 'Have you ever been to Moti Mahal? Eaten tandoori chicken?' I said no. 'Lets go', he said.

After guiding the driver through various meandering roads, he said 'Dariyagunj – Moti Mahal, yes, it's here.' He led us to the narrow staircase towards the terrace, avoiding the main hall. It looked like a *dhaba* (a wayside restaurant), with steel and wooden furniture. He ordered two tandoori chickens. While eating, he commented, 'Chicken from the mountains, only bones. No meat but very tasty, I like it.'

I was surprised to see how native Corbusier had become. Relishing the most rustic, almost rundown atmosphere of this very famous restaurant in Delhi. Looking at his watch he stood up, walked down. About to board the Jeep, he stopped and said, 'Au revoir, mon petit Doshi', then suddenly left, full of emotions and love. That was in 1964. This is my Indian guru. Formal, informal, lovable and detached, all in one.

For Louis Kahn too, Corbusier was like a distant guru. Shyness made him avoid meeting Corbusier. This is like the *Mahabharata* story of Eklavya who gave his thumb to his distant guru Dronacharya. Remembering this, I felt these two giants should meet. I wanted to schedule their meeting soon. Unfortunately on 27 August, 1965 Corbusier died swimming. A few days later I was in Philadelphia. On arrival, I went to meet Lou at his studio. No sooner than I entered, he said, 'Did you hear?' 'Yes,' I said 'I was in Paris two days ago. He is no more.' Lou said, 'All these years I worked and felt his presence, and wondered if he would have liked my work, if he saw it.' After a pause with watery eyes Lou said, 'Now for whom shall I work?'

This is how Gurus are remembered.

GIVE TIME A BREAK

1998

Land – ownership & enrichment?

canvas, cloth, tin roof
mud walls
charpoy
1st stage

2nd stage
addition of new temporary room

Terrace
3rd stage
enclosure of court

courtyard verandah
cluster of homes / extended family.

village as new settlements in organized sectors

I was born into an extended Hindu family. Several generations lived together; some members were 80 years old and some just a few days old. Birth, growth and death were recurring and natural events. So were the celebrations of festivals, birth ceremonies and extended rituals with trips together to temples or pilgrimage places. Everyone accepted and shared these inevitable events. Days, months and seasons passed through good times and bad. Over time, changes in lifestyles, changes or breaks in the social, economic and cultural structure within the household became a living part of each of us.

With the evolution, the character, form, and style of the house in which we lived was also transformed. It grew organically, from just a few rooms to many and from one floor to several. Modified functions and revised movements appeared strange, and at times new, yet they were accepted and absorbed naturally. The expanding structure of the house and its evolving functions were like a big sponge – porous and forever absorbing, constantly providing us with new spatial and aesthetic surprises. However, the focal points – the kitchen, the dining room, and the prayer room maintained their positions, dominating the overall ambience and remaining the foundation for the shifting plan and functions. Such continuous evolutions and transformation have become part and parcel of my perceptions of life as well as my aesthetic experience.

I often went with others to nearby villages and temples to attend various ceremonies. Even though the rituals appeared to be similar, their purpose, manner of performance, scale and location differed. These took place in diverse places: on a river bank, in the open court of a house, or within the precinct of a shrine. These scattered events, set in both modest and profusely decorated settings, did not seem odd, but rather gave one a chance to learn more about uncertainty and constant flux.

The rituals emphasised the sacredness of each event instantly and deepened the understanding of our relationship to the cosmos. With these tenuous connections of the unknown, the newly acquired sanctity of a normal space and the shifting of local time to cosmic time, the externality was dematerialised. Everything became part of the ritual with the chanting and soon the invisible but omnipresent Gods arrived. They participated and, after the chanting of the final *aarti*, they blessed each individual present and departed. Though these rituals lasted between 15 minutes to more than eight hours, we did not realise the passage of time, space or the individual. Psyche, emotions and faith combined to make each event and experience mythical.

I now sense the how and why of this continuing acceptance of life. It is actually the experience of constant sharing. Sharing multiplied the effects of joyous events and diminished those of sad ones. It added new dimensions to our understanding of life as a constantly turning wheel or a broken circle, whether we performed the planned or the unexpected religious or social ceremonies. Living together helped us understand the uncertainties in life, the successes and failures. These increased our tolerance and changed the perception of life from material to spiritual values. Even the conception of life after death and reincarnation brought about hope. An unending chain of construction and destruction, where the 'present' is only a phase in transition. These experiences made me realise that life is full of surprises and paradoxes. Everything that occurred in the past can happen again in another time, place and form. Once past, events become unrealities, memories or visions. Such endless fluctuation of experience between oneself and others, of the immediate world and beyond, of good and bad, and then and now, are simply God revealing and concealing his game, his *lila*.

Traditional Hindu architecture, which expresses through movement – whether fast or slow, with several pauses, is perceived not only as a part of this instant or eternity, but as an intimate experience. Architecturally, the broken wheel of time is expressed as a sequence of juxtaposed long and short corridors with a variety of pauses, scales, interspersed courtyards, and unexpected visual barriers, including changes in structural expression or in the quality of light.

Likewise, in traditional Indian architecture, each space can be perceived independently to complete a unique experience. One can be transformed through a proactive dialogue with space and time. One can cross a threshold into another space, another time, and another phase of psychological and spiritual experiences. Walls, columns, surfaces, rhythms, light, etc, are instruments that activate these spaces. Such experiences can be had throughout India, in places both small and large, and in social, religious, or royal complexes. In these complexes there exists a natural pattern in which the normative activities connected to specific functions are transcended and surrounded by an immense number of peripheral links and areas with no apparent function. Even in the conventional temple complex, the zone of activity and the interaction with the participants is marginal. While the open, pillared *sabhamandap* invites assembly, the enclosed, dark *girbhagriha* admits few, thus establishing an inner awareness of silence, void, and timelessness. However, when a devotee undertakes the ritualistic circumambulation on the plinth around the external face of the shrine of the hidden deity, his perception of time and space is transformed, even though the physical space remains the same.

When I visit the Meenakshi Temple at Madurai, a vast complex built over seven centuries, the spatial experiences continually reveal the duality of life through simultaneous coexistence of the extremes, namely space organisation characterised by the informal, as well as formal, structured with loose, and finite with infinite. These spatial attributes are also intrinsic to traditional towns and villages of India. The built forms and open spaces enrich both the private and public realms. Corridors of various scales are designed to instantly recall our ancient history through columns or walls elaborately decorated with stories and myths that immediately connect to other worlds with different times, even though the clock continues to tick normally.

The varied sizes, scales, and typologies of the open and semi-covered courtyards extend my vision to the eternal passage of the sun or the moon, the changing patterns of the starlit sky and the rhythms of the seasons. The saturated, diverse, and simultaneous experiences at the temple, as well as the deities in the niches of the walls surrounding the shrines, intercept my movement through the depiction of social context similar to those in towns. Nevertheless, these diverse experiences do not distract me from the goal, instead they simultaneously connect me to the main and multiple centres and peripheries in this complex. Strangely, this vast complex becomes condensed into one experience, its diversity appearing simultaneously, both close and far. For example, watching a statue of a deity hidden in the corner of a dark room adjacent to the corridor, I constantly sense the presence of the main deity across a great distance and through the layers that surround it. A universal energy seems to be generated by the dynamic relationships among solids and voids, built and unbuilt.

Another significant and completely different architectural example is the observatory at Jaipur, known locally as Jantar Mantar, which implies magical contraptions. Here, the visitor enters into a totally different time frame. All of the architectural manifestations are sculptural interpretations of scientific instruments employed to measure cosmic time through the movements of the planets and stars. These devices represent a condensation of all celestial movements in a permanent stage set of precisely located and oriented architectural forms. The casual observers may experience the enigmatic quality of their geometry, but for an inquiring mind, the shadows moving over time, somehow convey silent but certain connections with the sky, the cosmos, and the larger order of time.

Yet another example is the Islamic complex at Sarkhej, Ahmedabad, built around 1466. Here, a summer palace, a mosque, and several tombs are organised around a tank. It is the most frequented monument in the city. Some visit this complex simply to go to the mosque, some only to the tombs, while others sit under the pavilions in the arid climate. In the end, they all sit around the steps that enclose the vast water tank, performing the daily chores of washing clothes or bathing. Even though the complex has designated areas for the tomb, the mosque and the pavilions, there are several unassigned, in-between spaces that have become unique, allowing for spontaneous activities ever-changing with seasons,

Old city of Ahmedabad + The
created the "Brand Ahm
made each citze
Body

Technology

Time
Energ
Spir

Matter

Pas

Save Time + Energy
Dynamic - C

...titution of Mahajans
...nd" = Public-Private Partnership
...ealthy, wealthy, wise
along with a socially secure
community.

Environment

Mind

Spirit — Energy

Matter

"Hour Glass"

...create Biodiverse
...xisting world

SSli
Dec 2/08

festivities and intensity of visitors. Rather than physical architectural linkages, the visual, emotional and psychological connections have become important and contribute to the popularity and compelling force of this complex.

The building has a strong relation to the sun, the moon and the water. The famous step wells that connect the changing levels of drinking water are our unique architectural monuments celebrating the presence of and access to water. Narrow, long and often more than five floors deep, these underground wells are located mostly in hot, dry climates where the water level changes drastically during the monsoon and summer seasons. Going beyond mere functionality, the sequence and process of the task of fetching water is elaborately designed to exalt the ceremonial and sacred aspects of water. The introduction of several pauses and the provision of underground rooms are for resting and to accommodate gatherings away from the hot sun.

The passage of time is conveyed to the relaxing crowd through the daily movements of the sun and shadows, which filter through the lattice of beams and columns, as well as through the seasonally-changing water level.

In this ceremoniously designed, inclined and horizontal space, planned and unplanned encounters with other community members encourage one to discuss – and absorb or efface personal experiences of daily family life. In the shadows and the silhouettes against the sky, one discovers the story of a period full of myths and realities. In the Indian subcontinent, towns and cities that grew over time narrate similar physical and metaphysical stories. For example, the juxtaposition of linear, meandering streets with multifaceted, irregular open spaces at Delhi, Ahmedabad, and other cities, or the high plinths of the houses with deep verandas at Benares, or the open-sky terraces and extra large gargoyles in the desert of Jaisalmer, or the finely-carved *jharokhas* at Jaipur, Rajasthan, simultaneously express the need of a very complex way of life and the aspirations of a particular people and place. Layers of forms, surfaces and architectural styles vary in relation to climatic conditions, suggesting the continuity and prolongation of time. The architecture expresses a lifestyle that has existed and will exist as long as the context does.

While recalling these experiences, one realises how much one has drifted away from those so-called immeasurable activities and spaces that are essential to society's physical and social balance. It seems that we have to find ways to compel inhabitants to notice the changes in the seasons, the phases of the moon and their link to the rise and flow of tides, or the rising and setting of the sun in order to enable the inner self, once again, to perceive unpredicted pauses which contain timeless energy.

Measuring the utility of buildings by months or years does not reveal the quality of one's experience of a building. It is really a disconnected and personal, time-bound experience. If the design has provided for a separation of time zones, a layering of external and internal worlds, or alternate modes of movement with elements to slow down, break-up and change the course of the time and movement relationship, would that not provide choices and unexpected joys? Does the absence of a sustained order not lead to more memorable experiences? This is always true of great architecture. Sadly, it is not true of our present time. With the passage of time, new dimensions have entered our perceptions. Our measure of time is accelerating and events are now coupled with rapid change and uncertainty. The relationship of man to built form has become transitory and identity has become synonymous with quick, result-oriented action. Symbols are now dependent upon a constantly changing and increasingly uncertain world view.

Against this myopic world view and the resulting well-structured, extremely regulated, mechanised architectural spaces, the only constant that can recover our sensibilities is the introduction of the pause, the 'gap', or unexpected, ambiguous link. This gap, or 'open-ended ambiguity', through its momentary sense of repose in time and reorientation of space, helps counteract stressful activity. In architecture, this gap or pause is the unassigned, loosely superimposed space, the corner or corridor or irregular courtyard accidentally discovered. In these spaces, use is undefined and choice is unlimited. The spaces may not have tangible, measurable or material value, but they have a permanent experiential and immeasurable value because they contain the possibility of spontaneity.

In the academic and cultural complexes and the townships that I have designed, I have included these currently ignored architectural elements, whose only functions are to break the circle of time, to allow opportunity to pause, meander, or just to go astray. Because time can stop. And when time is still, we can discover the joys of getting lost in space, in time, or in a place, effacing the traces of a linear, stressful life by registering the changing nuances of shadows and rhythms in space, the quality of light, colour, texture or the sound of falling rain or the smell of flowers. This in turn connects us to our primordial, timeless self. This is the challenge I have taken up in my projects. In our Aranya housing for the 'have-nots' at Indore, a multidimensional use of time and resources was employed. To encourage unexpected but accepted participation, the form and pattern of flexible dwellings with growth potential is integrated with the street patterns.

Pauses in the form of open spaces are provided, allowing the residents to choose time, contact, or activity before reaching a destination. As a result, Aranya offers residents a choice to live at either the pace of a village or small town, or at that of a neighbourhood on the fringe of a metropolis.

Similar to Fatehpur Sikri near Agra or the Meenakshi Temple at Madurai, unassigned open and semi-open architectural connections mark the passage of time at the Indian Institute of Management in Bangalore. Over 20 years in the making and with several directors modifying the academic programme, an architecture of uncertainty helped to add new dimensions to the flexibility of the campus. passage along the spine is modulated with changing light, spaces and scales in the covered and semi-covered pergolas, that encourage the academicians to pause and reconsider the existing and new interactive modes of communication. Sangath distils both the experiences of my ancestral home and those in Le Corbusier's architectural studio in Paris. Its form and plan raise haunting questions about form, formality and ambiguity. To reach the partially-buried design studio, one has to pass through several meandering open and enclosed passages that are intermingled with natural elements such as the sun, the moon, water, flora and fauna. When passing from one point to another, one is compelled to recognise the connections between the manmade and the cosmic and to acquire a glimpse of the enigmatic or the immeasurable, the essential parameter of creation.

Underground, dimly lit and unfathomable space is what Amdavad ni Gufa (*gufa* literally means cave) means. Its fluid space, which has now become a natural girbhagriha, or 'golden womb', is where one is able to discover previous births and reincarnations. Such unexpected experiences make one ask: Who am I? Where do I come from? What time is it? How much and whose time do we have? Yet these questions become irrelevant as one delves deeper, as in a yogic trance. In the gufa, the past, present and future are fused into a seamless continuum. There is no beginning and no end: in that space time stands still.

ACKNOWLEDGEMENTS

First and foremost, I would like to express my deepest gratitude to Balkrishna Doshi, who supported the book project from the very beginning and agreed to give an interview linking the thoughts of his past writings with the present.

My appreciation also goes to Khushnu Hoof, who helped me along with the Vastushilpa Foundation, and all the other copyright holders.

Finally, my special thanks go to the initiator of the book, Cristina Steingräber, who made the creation and publication of the book possible. I would also like to thank the art director, Julia Wagner, and Claire Cichy, for their excellent work.

Vera Simone Bader

QUO VADIS? [13]

| Where do we go ? |

Bibliography and Credits

Doshi, B., *Regionality,* World Design Conference, Tokyo, Japan, 1960.
© Vastushilpa Foundation for Studies and Research in Environmental Design

'Indian Architecture and Its Criticism', in *Cultural Forum* – Criticism in India, Ministry of Science Research and Cultural Affairs, Ahmedabad, 1965.
© Vastushilpa Foundation for Studies and Research in Environmental Design

Rural Housing, All India Radio, March 1970.
© Vastushilpa Foundation for Studies and Research in Environmental Design

Values and Scales. Musings of an Architect, Second Iran International Conference of Architecture (IICA), Tehran, Iran, 1974.
© Vastushilpa Foundation for Studies and Research in Environmental Design

Limits of City Growth, Cairo Symposium, Cairo, Egypt, 1978.
© Vastushilpa Foundation for Studies and Research in Environmental Design

Architecture and Attitudes, Unido-ICSIID Meeting on Design for Development, National Institute of Design, 14–24 January 1979.
© Vastushilpa Foundation for Studies and Research in Environmental Design

'Toward an Appropriate Living Environment: Questions on Islamic Development', in Safran, L. (ed.), *Places of Public Gatherings in Islam,* The Aga Khan Award for Architecture, 1980, pp. 135–137.
© Aga Khan Trust for Culture

'Identity in Architecture: Contemporary Pressures and Tradition in India', in *Architectural Association Quarterly,* vol. 13, no. 1, October 1981, pp. 19–22.
© Vastushilpa Foundation for Studies and Research in Environmental Design

Doshi, B., Chauhan, M. and Parikh, P., 'Vohra Houses in Gujarat', in Petruccioli, A. (ed.), *Environmental Design: Journal of the Islamic Environmental Design Research Centre,* Rome, Carucci Editore, 1984, pp. 52–63.
© Attilo Petruccioli

'Cultural Continuum and Regional Identity in Architecture', in Powell, R. (ed.), *Regionalism in Architecture,* The Aga Khan Award for Architecture/Concept Media Pte, 1985, pp. 87–91.
© Aga Khan Trust for Culture

Doshi, B. and Chauhan, M., 'Learning from Old Jaipur', in *Journal of the Indian Institute of Architects,* vol. 52, nos. 3 & 4, September–December 1987, pp. 30–35.
© Vastushilpa Foundation for Studies and Research in Environmental Design

'Between Notion and Reality', Borden, C.M. (ed.), *Contemporary Indian Tradition: Voices on Culture, Nature, and the Challenge of Change,* Washington, D.C., Smithsonian Institution Press, 1989, pp. 335–353, reprinted with the permission of Smithsonian Institution.
© Smithsonian Institution

Growth, Change and Development in Urban Centres, lecture in Jakarta, 1996.
© Vastushilpa Foundation for Studies and Research in Environmental Design

Le Corbusier: The Indian Incarnation, lecture at Colloque Le Corbusier Messager Fondation Suisse, Paris, France, 2–5 December 1996, in *Balkrishna Doshi, Talks,* Ahmedabad, 2012.
© Vastushilpa Foundation for Studies and Research in Environmental Design

Give Time a Break, Eighth Annual Anytime Conference, Ankara, Turkey, 15–17 June 1998, in *Balkrishna Doshi, Talks,* Ahmedabad, 2012.
© Vastushilpa Foundation for Studies and Research in Environmental Design, and Cyntia Eisenmann

Photo Credits

Photographs on pages 17, 21, 26
© Vastushilpa Foundation for Studies and Research in Environmental Design

Editor: Vera Simone Bader

Idea and Concept: Cristina Steingräber

Project Management: Cristina Steingräber
with Daniil Aksenov, Linda Hornung

Proofreading: Claire Cichy, Cristina Steingräber

Art Direction: Julia Wagner, grafikanstalt

Reproductions: Peter Maus

Printing and Binding: DZA Druckerei zu Altenburg GmbH, Altenburg

© 2019 ArchiTangle GmbH, and the authors

Published by
ArchiTangle GmbH
Meierottostrase 1
10719 Berlin
Germany
www.architangle.com

ISBN 978-3-96680-001-3